THIS BOOK WILL SAVE YOUR LIFE!

It's about reclaiming our increasingly deteriorating civilization through non-violent rebellion and revolution.

We're in trouble! You KNOW this, I don't need to sell it. Are you unemployed? Losing your house? Unable to gas your car? Are you hungry? Is watching the news getting you down? Is it getting you nowhere? Or... do you just have a **bad feeling** about your world but don't quite know why?... which is where I started. You could be in a position where you have your needs and wants met but are witnessing the implosion of the lives of those you know and love or even strangers. Wondering if and when it will affect you too... Then there's the unenviable position of being one of the *'bad guys' but* feeling guilty. Worst case... are you a *bad guy* AND simply don't care?

Chances are you are in the list above in some variation or combination. We all are. And take notice that NONE of the above are desirable positions. This is simply because a *broken world* is **no fun** for anyone!

This book is about rebirth, second chances, getting a 'do over'! It's about *'frolicking in the garden'* as opposed to *'crawling in the desert'*. It's about:

Learning, living and loving!

BUY, BORROW OR STEAL THIS BOOK!! IT'LL SAVE ALL OF OUR LIVES!!

This book is for **EVERYONE!** Man, Woman, Child and Teen; Hero, Villain, Everyone in between!!!

FINALLY, a book about the *solution* to the *problem...* rather than another about the *problem* with *no solution!*

'World Repair Manual'

An Absolute MUST read! Best hour you ever spent!! OUTRAGIOUS!!!

To be read **over** and **over** and **over** again...

Orwell's *"Animal Farm"* goes GLOBAL!
...*"1984"*comes 30 years late... with a *vengeance!*

The Donkey, The Elephant and The Lame Duck have gone the way of the Dinosaur... EXTINCT!! Check out the NEW Animals...

Lions Unite to Save the Sheep and Un'pack' the Wolves!!

It's NOT an 'Occupation', It's a 'Movement'!!

CONTROVERSIAL, THOUGHT PROVOKING, UNCONVENTIONAL

...out of the *'box'*, outside the *'nine dots'*...

A primer for spiritual, social and intellectual evolution.

Spiritually: Uplifting;

Emotionally: Heart Wrenching;

Intellectually: Stimulating;

Physically: Can't put it down!

A **signpost** up ahead reads: This way to the TRUTH... to FREEDOM...

'The Love Bomb': a weapon of mass construction *(WMC)*

It's the plan that came from **'outer space'**...

The Embodiment of Idealism

The End is Near; Time is Spare; Evolution is imminent;

SO BE PREPARED!!!

Lions are gathering at lions-unite.org

Join the revolution!

"Single acts of tyranny may be ascribed to the accidental opinion of the day; but a series of oppressions, begun at a distinguished period, and pursued unalterably through every change of ministers too plainly proves a deliberate, systematic plan of reducing us to slavery."

-Thomas Jefferson

Planet Of The Sheep

Blueprint for Revolution 2012

By: GG Lionhart

aka

"The Little Boy Who Cried Wolf"

Clover Publishing

Let this be dedicated to them both.

To those who forge the weapon,

Trusting in strength,

And those who renounce it,

Trusting in faith.

Those who lived through the time of trial warn us:

Better to have and not require

Than to grasp and find the scabbard empty.

But let us never cease to ask

If the time has come

When we no longer need the sword at all.

David Poyer *(Tomahawk 1998)*

For Deanna and Emily

For

Joshua, Ryan and Cody

Gregory, Jayson and Garrett

Amanda and Nicholas

Maurianne and Roxanne

Alma, Alicia, Monica and Eric

and for all of the young people who deserve
to inherit a beautiful, functional planet and
society.

Welcome to the *'flock'*,

welcome to the *'pride'*!!

Goodbye to the *'pack'*...

ACKNOWLEDGMENTS

Very special thanks to my traveling companion and mentor:
Colonel & Professor **Frank W. Snell** (deceased)

It all began on a hot July night in 2006 in Costa Rica onboard the
Windjammer Barefoot Cruise ship *'Legacy'*. Sixty passengers in fairly
close quarters for a week doing lots of talking and interacting but the
subject always revolving around and returning to politics and current
events. I hate that stuff but I was trapped... so I joined in. I spoke
with **Lisa** until late into the night one night and consequently, this
project was *'born'*. It finally happened **Lisa!**

Then I spent some time in Europe to get an *'overseas'* point of view on
America as well as the rest of the world. I stepped *'out of the box'*.
Danielle, Richard, Maurianne and especially **Roxanne** had a huge
influence on me. Also, gave me a *'home'* away from home.

I went to Maui in May 2008 to *'lay down'* the first draft. I stayed in
Tom's living room for three days of solid typing. **Sheri** let me print out
the fifty page rough proof at her house. Two complete strangers
invited me into their homes to draft up the plan. They even threw me
an unforgettable birthday party. ...There's the very *'model'* I'm
writing about..! Thank you very much.

In the almost four years since the Maui trip, I persisted in toting
around the manuscript and continued to research, edit, think,
observe, evolve and procrastinate. I called it *"watching the
'window'."* I've also been working intimately with my own 'fear
management'. This is a SCARY PROJECT! Well, the *'window'* is here
so I HAVE to *'get over it'*... Here it is... the 'moving target'... the
perpetual 'work in progress'... the ***manifesto!*** Finished.

I give thanks to **GOD** for His master plan that encompasses and
overrides all of our *'sub'*-plans and petty schemes.

Thank you to all the **Human Beings** of Planet Earth. We're a *'living laboratory'* of infinite possibility! Hang in there... MANIFEST!

I send thanks 'back' to the **American Founding Fathers** who *'got it'*... Sorry guys, we *'lost it'* and need to *'re-get it'*...

Thanks **George Lucas.** Artist and genius at packaging & delivering the *'message'*... you *'get it'!*

Thank you **Dennis.** You provided a *'ringside view'* for me to observe a *'cog'* in the *'big wheel,* a *'base of ops'* behind the *'lines'*...

Thanks go to my friend **James.** Philosopher & spiritual mentor. You manage to keep me grounded AND unbalanced... I grow...

Thanks **Eduardo** for encouraging me to be all I can be.

Thank you **Mykee:** artist extraordinaire. You provided moral support, technical support and a WORLD CLASS cover!

Thanks to **Rupert** for the self-publishing advice and assistance.

Thank you (Annie's) mom, **Louise** in So Cal. Yes, I WAS working while sunbathing in the back yard...

Thanks **Buttons** (the cat) for patiently competing with my laptop

Also, huge thanks go out to **Annelous** for your unwavering love, patience and support! You *"pussycat"* lover, you!

Thanks to my daughter, **Deanna.** Rebellion definitely runs in the family... as does the love. You 'fueled' ALL of this...

But mostly, thank you **Mom!** You believe in me...unconditionally.

Planet of the Sheep

Table of Contents   **10**

Preface *(previews of coming attractions)*   **13**

Prelude to Part 1 *(synopsis)*   **19**

PART ONE *(Fiction section)*   **21**

Prelude to Part 2

PLANET OF THE SHEEP

    (a parable in the making)   **23**

PART TWO *(Non-Fiction section)*   **35**

Foreword *(preludes and parallels)*   **37**

Introduction

    (what's it all about)   **39**

Chapter 1: **Rebel with a Cause**

    (a little bit about me)   **49**

Chapter 2: **The State of the Union**

    (a little bit about us)   **55**

Chapter 3: **Critical Mass**

    (a trip to the crystal ball)   **61**

Planet of the Sheep

Chapter 4: **Birth of a Revolution**

(your mission when you accept it) **73**

Chapter 5: **A Call to Action**

(execution without death) **83**

Chapter 6: **Out with the Old**

(no encore, please) **105**

Chapter 7: **Transitioning**

(growing pains) **109**

Chapter 8: **Paradigm Shift**

(keeping the peace) **121**

Chapter 9: **A New Eden**

(life in the garden) **125**

Epilogue **127**

Afterword

(back to the parable) **131**

Appendix **133**

Further Research and Viewing **154**

Contact & Order Information **160**

Planet of the Sheep

"The only sure bulwark of continuing liberty is a government strong enough to protect the interests of the people, and a people strong enough and well enough informed to maintain its sovereign control over the government."

-Franklin D. Roosevelt

Idealism def:

i·de·al·ism [**ahy**-dee-*uh*-**liz**-*uh* m] *noun*

1. the cherishing or pursuit of high or noble principles, purposes, goals, etc.

2. the tendency to represent things in an ideal form, with emphasis on values.

3. Utopian philosophy.

Preface

(previews of coming attractions)

What you're about to read is not a book, it's a **manifesto.** A plan of action. It's also a true story about the past, present and future of our world. It's not for some, **it's for all**. Every age, every race, every religion, every *human* being alive and yet to be born. This is a story that will change our society. Rock our world... back ON to its axis. This is a plan of action to save the world. **Everyone** has a part to play. A mission. It's called a *"manifesto"* because it's intention is to *'manifest'* positive results.

This plan has been mapped out in very simple, right to the point terms. No fluff and no *'filler'*. These concepts have been refined and simplified in accordance with **'Occam's razor': the law of economy. This states that the simplest and most obvious solution is usually the correct one. The best one.**

This plan is for readers and non-readers alike. As mentioned, it is for everyone. Non-readers will get the story too;

Planet of the Sheep

either through audio, video, or handed down by *'word of mouth'*. Everyone will know this story, join the cause, and participate in the reclaiming, repairing, and rebuilding of our damaged, burned out civilization. It's also about **freedom.** Not the kind that is supposedly *'granted'* to us by our government or *'won'* in wars with other countries and cultures. It's the type of freedom which is our **natural God given birthright.** And we will have it by simply standing up and claiming it. To do this will require a little faith and a lot of courage. **Everyone** will wear the title **Superhero**. Are you intrigued? Stay tuned.

In Part 1, the plan begins with a simple metaphoric parable designed to illustrate the point of our plight. Look between the lines. See if you can make the connection. Understand and be alarmed by the parallels. Decide in advance what your position currently is and what role you intend/wish to play. This plan is all about choices. YOU get to choose. So choose wisely.

I wrote my first poem for you:

Planet of the Sheep

"Be it villain or hero, foe or friend, every player will win in the end. And if the choices are made to not play at all, then all is for naught as, in the end, we fall".

The fall of civilization as we know it, that is... we're '*in'* it now. It's not too late to reverse it. This will require full participation. This is the ultimate '*all or nothing'* scenario. The game to end all games. Is there even a question whether or not to play? You all know this to be true. The writing is on.... your faces. The fear is in your conversations. The truth is in our hearts.

There's a popular song titled *"Waiting On The World To Change."* It's a nice song but... if you happen to subscribe to this passive philosophy, you might find yourself '*waiting'* for a very long time. Worse still, the world will probably change in ways you don't like. Especially if it *"stays the course"* it's currently on. Have you heard that last '*Presidential'* quote before..?

In Part 2, we get real. We leave the mythical '*planet of the sheep'* and emerge in a very real present day *Earth* where a frighteningly similar situation is in progress...

In the first chapters, you will learn a

Planet of the Sheep

little about me and a lot about my motivation for starting this rebellion. In the middle chapters, you will be exposed to the plan itself. Finally, in the latter chapters, you will understand the vision that we all as peaceful, loving beings share hidden beneath our fear and realize the possibility of bringing this vision to fruition. Of finally creating and embracing the illusive... *Utopia.* Manifesting the legendary *Shangri-La.*

At the back of the book. as well as interspersed, you will find an excellent, diverse and highly recommended collection for further reading and viewing *(bibliography)* from which this entire project developed and evolved. All the research has already been done. The *'problem'* has been thoroughly identified. I'm not here to reiterate all of it, just to *'boil it down'.* Consider me the *'glue'...* the *'magnifying glass'.* The *'translator'.*

This plan is to bring together not only this enormous existing body of information, but the huge *'family'* of *peace mongers* that is already *'out there'* attempting to make a difference. All that we're lacking is organization and coordination... on a global scale.

Planet of the Sheep

Don't ignore or take these concepts lightly. They are very powerful. They can and will make the difference... *'fuel'* the change required to pull our planet out of its *disastrous orbit.* Use the books and videos I've listed to supplement... to fill in the gaps and complete this manuscript. Call it *'homework'!* Visit the website. That's WHY it's called **further research** and I'll indicate the ones that are **crucial**. INFORMATION IS POWER! Allow them to get you as fired up as they did me. They will **educate, motivate and anger** you. These resources will arm you to implement the change that **is required** in our society right now! All I have done is simplify and refine them to have a single impact point.

Important note about how to read this book: Part of my writing *'style',* is that I use plenty of *'italicized'* words and phrases with *'apostrophes around them'.* These emphasized areas usually indicate a *'deeper or double meaning'...* sort of a *'slow down and think about it flag'.* When I use triple dots... it means 'you finish the thought or sentence. When I use **bold** or ALL CAPS, it means **'louder'** or **stronger** emphasis... it also draws the eye to important sections... I've

Planet of the Sheep

basically done the highlighting FOR you!

This book was written to/for EVERYONE. It was very challenging because I had to keep it simple enough for the layman yet interesting and thought provoking enough to keep the intellectual engaged... as well as everyone else in between. I'm *'playing'* to ALL denominators. Children NEED to get this. Older people need it. People of every I.Q. and physical ability. Rich AND poor, mean and nice... Race, religion and culture. Clubber, cultist and *'cavedweller'*... EVERYONE!

It's a quick read. Read it multiple times. But mostly, DO the *'further research'* homework. It's ALL good stuff!! *...otherwise I wouldn't have included it...!!*

And now...

'On with the show'!

Prelude to part 1

Planet of the Sheep Synopsis

Planet of the sheep is a story about a simple society that becomes corrupt and then redeems itself. It's about how a few individuals can, through selfishness and greed, take an entire planet down the wrong path into chaos and, ultimately, destruction. It's a story of hope where the oppressed can organize and rise up to defeat the wasters and reclaim and repair their society. It is a story about us.

Planet of the Sheep

"But the wolves are so much stronger than us and meaner and have all the claws..."

-Little Blackie

PART ONE

Fiction Section

Planet Of The Sheep

A Parable

Planet of the Sheep

*"The **truth** is mightier than the **tooth**."*

-Little Blackie

"During times of universal deceit, telling the truth becomes a revolutionary act."

-George Orwell

Prelude to part 2

Planet Of The Sheep

(a parable in the making)

"Once upon a time...

There was a planet full of lambs. It was a peaceful planet. The lambs were herbivores and the planet was green with fresh clover on every hill. They grazed and multiplied and grew up into fat, content sheep. A whole planet full of sheep. Happily grazing and sharing their clover. No worries.

One day a remarkable thing happened. One of the sheep shed its skin and underneath was a wolf. It was a *'wolf in sheep's clothing'* so to speak. The wolf immediately sized up the situation and realized he was different than the sheep, in looks but also in habits. The clover didn't taste good to the wolf. It didn't take long for him to figure out that the sheep did. The wolf had to be very careful, however, so that the happy, unassuming sheep wouldn't notice this predicament. The sheep accepted the wolf's presence because the wolf never did anything *un-sheeplike* to rouse their suspicion... except that he ate and slept in a cave. But they were too busy grazing on fresh, plump clover to care.

Over time, more wolves came out of the flock and moved to the cave and secretly preyed upon the hapless flock of sheep. Soon, the wolves realized that they needed to get organized or the sheep would notice the increasing numbers of the wolves as well as their own decreasing numbers. Over time the sheep looked up from their grazing and noticed the ever growing pack of wolves and grew curious. They asked about their looks and they asked about their habits.

Planet of the Sheep

The wolves lied to the sheep and gained their confidence. And made their plans. The sheep went back to their clover.

The wolves secretly began raising sheep for food. They especially liked the feisty little lambs and few ever became fully grown. None ever learned what life was like in the pastures outside the cave. The wolves were very careful to keep their secret. They regularly received a generous portion of clover from the sheep as a gift. Little did the sheep know that the clover was being consumed by the hidden lambs and not the wolves. All in the world seemed good.

One day, a careless wolf was seen killing a lamb. The sheep were shocked and confused and asked the wolves why this had happened. The wolves lied to the sheep. They told them that some wolves were unstable and needed to be controlled by the other wolves. The wolves promised to protect the sheep from this 'bad' group. The sheep were grateful and went back to their grazing.

The wolves multiplied profusely over the years and their appetite grew accordingly. They needed more and more clover. The lambs were eating it up faster than the sheep could deliver it. The sheep were becoming suspicious that there were now so many wolves around and alarmed that the once lush green fields were beginning to grow sparse. The clover was going out faster than it was coming in.

The problem didn't go un-noticed by the wolves either. They tried alternative food sources on the lambs. Things like crabgrass and thistly swamp plants. The lambs suffered but ate. They grew up thinner and tougher and the wolves began to miss the meatier meals they used to enjoy. They began to sneak the occasional sheep out of the flock and have it conveniently disappear without explanation. The ravenous wolves were like the sheep. They were so caught up in the feasting that they didn't see past their own contentment. Didn't see that, through their gluttony, their secret was being revealed. The sheep eventually saw the truth but the wolves, locked in their long practiced behaviors, continued to oppress the sheep and pretend that they still had *'the wool over their eyes'.* The sheep, however, had had enough.

Now, sheep can get pretty riled up... but truth be told, they're natural followers. Even with the horrible truth descending upon them like the putrid breeze wafting down from the wolf caves in the hills, the sheep were helpless to act. They're sheep. They eat clover. They follow.

The situation got worse as the clover got more scarce. The sheep started fighting amongst themselves. Sheep started hoarding clover. Not sharing. Some starved. A lot of stockpiled clover went rancid and started a disease among the sheep. Even the wolves were catching the disease. It grew into a plague. Other types of animals started to appear to 'clean up' the dead. It seemed like nature sensed the need and provided the necessary 'links' to keep the circle of life going. *Omnivores.*

Over time, the disease became checked but the scavengers now needed a new food source. The balance became more precarious and the sheep started relying on the wolves to police the scavengers. A vicious circle developed where friends were allied with enemies and resources continued to dwindle, and the lies continued to flow. The oppression forged ahead like the hungry impulsiveness and determination of a starving pup. The wolves were so satiated from their gluttonous reign that they were oblivious to the awakening that was happening around them. The sheep were not eating clover anymore, they were discussing...

...And discussing... and discussing. Sheep only know how to follow. This was going to go nowhere. Then a miracle happened. One of the smarter, more outspoken sheep lost its skin and underneath was a new animal. It was golden in color and, alarmingly, had some equipment similar to the wolves. Namely, lots of sharp edges. And a voice that was thunderous. The eyes, however, were kind and intelligent. The sheep asked about its looks and its habits. Even though their stomachs were starting to cry out for clover.

"I am a lion. I have been living among you and learning about your peaceful lifestyle. I've also been studying the tyranny that you've been subjected to. I'm appalled that one species has the cruelty and shortsightedness to treat another the way those wolves have treated you sheep. I come from a species that emphasizes family values over gang mentality. Sharing over taking. And most important of all, protecting the young and the weak. We are lions and we care about our world and our brothers and cousins."

"What about those claws and teeth?" "You ARE somewhat similar to those wolves" Remarked the little black lamb in the front row. The huge lion replied, "We have learned that all animals were originally and are *naturally vegetarian."* *"We have explored this concept and actually find it quite satisfying. The thought of eating meat doesn't even appeal to us anymore."* The lion was on the level. They all munched some clover together and contemplated this new development.

Soon the lion spoke out and the sheep listened. They're not as good at listening as following, but listening is kind of like following so they listened... while they chomped. The lion said this: *"There are a lot of us lions and we are growing very concerned about what the wolves are doing to you sheep and to our world. We have analyzed the situation and decided on a remedy. The trick is that it will take full cooperation by all the sheep and eventually by all the wolves too. The magic of this solution is that no one gets left out. There's enough to go around for everyone with lots of clover*

Planet of the Sheep

left over." The sheep paused in their munching as their eyes grew round with visions of *'rolling in clover'.* Then they continued to listen... and chew. One track mind, those sheep. Got to love 'em though.

The lion said that the key to the plan was to take the wolves strength away, to get them out of the lamb raising business and teach them to eat normal food. To give them friendship and welcome them back into the flock... which is right where they started. But little Blackie's hoof shot up and he exclaimed *"But the wolves are so much stronger than us and meaner and have all the claws... How are we going to take their strength away?" "Easy"* the lion replied. *"Just stop feeding them."*

Wow! What a *planetshakingly* simple concept. As soon as the wolves ran out of lamb, they would be forced to eat the clover. They couldn't raise and eat the sheep anymore because the lions were now ON to the wolves' schemes. More and more lions were intermingling and actually cohabitating with the sheep. I guess you could say they were *'lying with the lambs'...* they were friends and they didn't have too much *pride* to show it. Also, these *'odd couple'* species had traits that were opposite and yet complimented each other. The lions were natural leaders yet compassionate and nurturing. The sheep, of course, were natural followers and somewhat high maintenance... They're really quite needy! It was a match made in *Eden's garden.*

The lions and sheep cut off the *'food supply'* to the wolves. The wolves had a fairly tough time of it. It wasn't easy giving up lamb. It wasn't easy giving up power and control. But they couldn't *'stand up'* to the combined effort of the *pride* and the *flock.* Some of them died, some rebelled and were exiled to a place 'reserved' for them to be together alone on their own. Most of them, however, changed their ways and transformed into good wolves. And you know what? Those wolves aren't such a bad lot after all. They're a little bit mangy and sometimes lazy... but they're happy and they're our friends now. And variety keeps our world interesting. We wouldn't want a planet full of just sheep...

Funny thing. The clover's coming back too.

The *(peacefully ever after)* End"

PART TWO

Non-Fiction Section

K.I.S.S.* Our World

A Plan for Freedom

"*If* **I** *can convert just* **one** *to love, it will make* **a** *difference;*

If **we** *can convert* **all** *to love, it will make* **the** *difference.*"

-An Anonymous Lion

*Keep It Simple, Share

Planet of the Sheep

"...he chose poorly..."

-The Knight from

"Indiana Jones and the Last Crusade"

Foreword

(preludes and parallels)

Now you've read the story of the **"Planet of the Sheep".** Keep it in mind as you process the following concepts. Perhaps you have already made your deductions and categorized yourself. You ARE in that story. All of you... unless you're an extra-terrestrial... or a rock. The question remains, *(and only YOU can answer it):* Are you a *sheep*, a *wolf*, a *lion,* or a *scavenger?* You ARE one of these already. What do you WANT to be? It's possible to 'change' your 'skin'... in fact, it's **required that you choose**. Just keep in mind, if you pick *wolf* or *scavenger*, it won't be long before you'll want to choose again...

The *lions* and the *sheep* are taking over.

Planet of the Sheep

"I see in the near future a crisis approaching that unnerves me and causes me to tremble for the safety of my country. As a result of the war, corporations have been enthroned and an era of corruption in high places will follow, and the money power of the country will endeavor to prolong its reign by working upon the prejudices of the people until all wealth is aggregated in a few hands, and the Republic is destroyed."

-Attributed to Abraham Lincoln

Introduction

(what's it all about?)

"We the people…" Or is it *"of the people, by the people, for the people?"* I think it's a little bit of all of the above. Whatever it was, it isn't anymore. The *'grand experiment'* created in America 230 or so years ago by its *rebellious* founding fathers, now has no resemblance to the original vision. In fact, if they could see us now, they would be ashamed and disgusted. *Turning in their graves* as some like to say. The original government was set up to serve and protect the people. Locally as well as internationally. Along the way the public leaders and their cronies got greedy and drunk on power and altered the rules of the game. Now *WE the people* serve the government and we require protection FROM them.

They know that we know this. That explains why they're working very hard towards massively arming themselves while incrementally disarming us.

Just like the slaveholders in our tainted history. The government is programming the

Planet of the Sheep

citizens to be subservient while they take and hold the position of master. If anyone chooses to disagree, another alteration *(amendment)* is created in the rules to protect and preserve the *master.*

Our original American *"Constitution"* and *"Bill of Rights"* were designed to protect us from a government run amok. Unfortunately the *'wolves'* were/are in charge of guarding the *'flock'.* **Big mistake.** They patiently and methodically altered the rules to suit their agenda. It has been done gradually over the decades and centuries and made so complex that we were basically lulled into always believing that they had our best interests at heart. Now, nobody knows what all the rules are, not even them.

Many of the citizens still believe in the sanctity of the government but they're becoming fewer and fewer. The writing is on the wall. The government has grown so blatant in its outright control and oppression that it simply cannot get away with *'sugarcoating'* it and serving it up to our gullible gullets anymore. We're catching on, yes, but we've also gotten ourselves in so deep that most have resigned themselves to the fact that it can't be reversed. I've been there. Apathetic. Not anymore though. To quote *Popeye: "I've had all I can stands and I can't stands no more."*

I call this irreversible phenomenon **"The Big Wheel."** It's huge and it will roll right over anything in its path. It's intimidating and actually quite powerful. I truly believe that the *'big wheel'* is unalterable but I also believe that it's NOT indestructible. Political candidates have been promising to alter its course for decades. I believe they couch this promise under the guise of *"change".* Let's rephrase that: *dis-guise* of *"change".* Have you heard this promise before? Have you been hearing it recently? Does it ever happen? Sure... for the worse. The change is always to the benefit of the promise makers and never to us, the promised ones. The *'big wheel'* just keeps on turning and will continue to do just THAT. Indefinitely. It's like a giant snowball rolling along sucking up everything in its path... and crushing everything else that doesn't suck.

We need a plan to *'break the wheel'.* It's the ONLY option. And this problem is not isolated to just the **USA.** **This plan**

Planet of the Sheep

INCLUDES: Africa, Asia, Europe, Australia, the Americas and every inhabited island and ship on the sea. All of the governments in the world have outgrown their usefulness. There was a time when there was a use for them. They helped to create infrastructure. Economical, physical and societal. That task has been accomplished and we're grateful to them for it. But now they're obsolete. A burden. Old and beyond the age of retirement. The *snowball* has evolved into an *avalanche* and we've been caught *yodeling* at the bottom of the mountain. It's time to jump on the ski lift and get on top of the situation. If we don't do something to *break the wheel,* we'll end up as *'road-kill'* and that'll be the end of the story.

Now, onward to the beginning of the story... and may you be frightened AND enlightened into action. Action being the only choice we have to save ourselves. Apathy and submission certainly won't.

Oh, before I start, a little bit more about the *'bad guy'.* The world's governments are a mixed blessing at best and the bane of our existence at worst. But government is NOT the villain. It's a tool. A mechanism being carefully and systematically utilized by a relatively small elitist group of individuals, commonly referred to as **Globalists**, to subjugate the general population into a two class society. One small class with the power, money and privilege and then everyone else who provides this for them. This *'group'* manipulates the governments, the media, the banks and the corporate sector to achieve their goals.

Think about it. By controlling the government, they control our freedom and rights. By controlling the media, they control information. What we believe and how we think stems from this. By controlling the banks and the money, they can manipulate the economy any way they wish. YIKES! We're suffering that one daily. Then, there's the corporate sector... the marketplace. Food, water, fuel, transportation, entertainment, etc. This covers our physical needs and wants. They really have us with this one. Very few can, or want to, exist outside *'the marketplace'* in our modern world.

By controlling these four major arenas, these **Globalists** can *'shape us'* into just about any type of society they desire. Their desire *(and master plan)* is nothing short of good old slavery... with a *'side'* of genocide. Yes, they don't want too many slaves, that would not be practical. Some will have to *'go'...* say about *80%* of them! This is a quintessential case of repeating some of our worst history. Are YOU prepared to serve the *'masters'?* Are you willing? Are you prepared for a premature demise...? I'm NOT! I won't! **The solution is simple, we ALL have to just say NO! We're NOT going to support their plan. NO WAY!!**

At this juncture, are you wondering why you haven't heard about these *elitists* and their master plan? It's because their biggest weapon is secrecy. They operate behind the scenes. They've been orchestrating our past, present and future for decades... perhaps centuries. Our best and only defense is to reveal them. To expose them to the whole world. Then to embrace non-violent non-compliance. We need to take the *'wind out of their sails'.* For shockingly revealing and believable information on this *'master plan'* of theirs, check out the film, *"Endgame, Blueprint for Global Enslavement"* by *Alex Jones.* You'll be *'changed'.*

Planet of the Sheep

Another *'weapon'* in their arsenal is really going to be a *'wake-up call'* for you if you really think about it. *They* are manipulating the four *'arenas'* mentioned above in such a way as to keep us all in **'crisis mode'**.

THIS IS CRITICAL FOR YOU TO UNDERSTAND!

We are so focused on our immediate situation and problems that we're completely oblivious to the *'big picture'*. Their master plan is so huge, complex and far-reaching that we simply don't believe it. They orchestrate these *arenas* in such a way that they never let them *'break'* completely. But they don't allow them to *'recover'* either. Our world remains in a precarious balance to keep us OFF balance, unfocused and unaware of what's going on behind the scenes.

Distracted. Disillusioned. Decoyed. Dis-informed, DISGUSTED... This is why our society appears to be stable even though it's very much not. I actually *admire* the ingenious, insidious and unscrupulous scope of their creepy plan... **this scares me the most.** This is VERY REAL!!!

Planet of the Sheep

What used to be called **"conspiracy theory"** is, in reality, **"conspiracy FACT"**. This term has lost a lot of credibility over time. Most think the *'theorists'* are *full of 'balony'*. This only proves that the *'brainwashing'* and the brilliant *cover stories* are working. **I used to be a skeptic, now I'm a believer. You need to open your mind and at least allow for the possibilities.** I'm addressing the *'sheep'* right now. You *'lions'* already know all of this... ...and, as for you *'wolves'*... time's up.

The **Globalists** are the *(very real)* threat. Now, a brief moment for some wild conjecture. PLEASE, *'humor me'* for just one paragraph...

Maybe not as real or imminent as the **Globalist** threat, but worthy of mention, I'll take this subject of the *enemy* to yet another level... so hold on to your *'spacesuit'*...

I've recently read an extremely interesting and convincing book titled *"The Day After Roswell" by Philip Corso*. It's written by a retired Army Colonel who was *allegedly* in charge of the artifacts *supposedly* recovered from the crash of an alien

Planet of the Sheep

spacecraft that happened at Roswell, New Mexico in *1948*. This *'E.T. story'* has been floating around for so long that, like me, **we've become conditioned to believe the *'cover (up) story'*...** that it never happened. As mentioned above, I'm as skeptical as the next scientific, thinking individual, but this book gave me serious doubts. It claims that protecting citizens from hostile extraterrestrials is the hidden agenda behind the decades long *Cold War* and *arms race.* The artifacts are also the source for much of our super-advanced technology and the reason the U.S. got such a huge lead on the rest of the world in this *arena.* Sound crazy? Read this compelling book and decide for yourselves. If it IS true, the Army did a great job of hiding it from us. They even hid it from most of the government right up to, and including, the Presidents. Done in the interest of protecting us from a truth they felt we couldn't handle but mostly to give them an advantage over, not only our *'enemies'*, but the other branches of the U.S. military. It's no secret there's considerable competition between them and the Army played it *'close to the vest'.* Is E.T. really out there? Are *'they'* a valid threat? If so, I can't think of a better motivation for pulling together as a society against an outside danger. But, for now, let's concentrate on the more immediate, addressable issues here on good ol' *Terra Firma* and *'cross that bridge'...* IF we come to it...

This leads me to my final point: **There is an even bigger *enemy... (the biggest)*** to be dealt with. This will require a more extensive description though so I'll save it for chapter 5. Be patient...

Now for a very important note: For the duration of this little adventure, take yourself **'out of the box'.** Pretend you're one of those *aliens* from another planet and here to observe our culture. Strip away your biases, prejudices and preconceptions. Absorb this information with new eyes. Unfortunately, most are unaware that they're *'brainwashed'.* That's the insidiousness of it all. Just assume that you are and start taking the *'action steps'.* You'll soon discover, as I did, that the more time you spend *'out of the box',* the more you'll become fully aware of the truth. The *'brainwashing'* WILL wear off. Choose to believe!

Join us *'lions'!*

Chapter 1:

Rebel with a Cause

(a little bit about me)

I was born a *Rebel*. From the day I attempted to slide down Grandma's stair banister and fell on my head *(against specific instruction to avoid such activity)* and woke up in the ambulance, to being the disobedient *'goof off'* of my scout troop. From my high school years as *'class clown'* and rebelling against everything my dad, the *'cop'*, stood for, through decades of *'flying below the radar'* of society, getting fat off of the system and living in forced denial of the state of my world.

As I slipped past fifty, I started to *'wake up'* and realize that the *'ride'* was becoming terribly precarious and I wasn't doing anything to contribute to the stabilization of my increasingly disintegrating world. Having lived my entire life as an anti-authoritarian, I've never had an interest in politics. I've always believed that government has grown so huge and out of control, that it could never be re-harnessed.

Planet of the Sheep

I never vote for this very reason. The futility of it. This perpetually recurring *'lack of choice'* syndrome. You know the old game: pick the lesser of two evils. I've actively avoided watching the news for years now. Of course, I still get enough news to know how much trouble we're in *(I have researchers studying it for me).*

So, here I am finding myself taking a hard look at the current state of affairs and growing very concerned. Seeing the need for some kind of workable strategy or plan. Credentials? What are those..? I'm no author and I'm certainly no political scientist. But my eyes, ears and brain work and so do most of yours. The important concept is to observe from *'outside the box'*. Look at the whole puzzle. Back off from those *'trees'*. To really *'get'* this stuff, you really have to concentrate on the **big picture**. More on this later.

I'm also a *Planner*. By nature and by trade. I plan people space for a living. I study people. Currently, my *'people'* are running out of *'space'*... literally and figuratively. We're suffocating... being suffocated... sinking fast. We NEED a plan. A

Planet of the Sheep

solution that's unconventional. Something that's never been tried before. A peaceful revolution on a global scale... a world-wide non-violent rebellion. I'm writing this to you now because I feel I've been in the rebellion business my whole life and I know the need when I see it. I also recognize that timing is everything and a *'window'* has opened. A vacuum has been created rendering us very vulnerable and highly susceptible to whichever influence rises and *'steps in'*. This phenomenon happened in Europe in *1939*. The results were catastrophic. We're currently positioned for a repeat performance. The *'bad guy'* is living among us waiting for this opportunity. Patiently watching for this window too. And planning. Bad guys don't rely on luck and they're not dumb. They plan too. This isn't *'rocket surgery'* folks. If we let them, they will take us on a ride through a Hell the likes of which we've never known. In today's small world and with the technology now available, brutal, oppressive slavery will be the only legacy our children will inherit. The bad guys are already in position. Before it's too late, we NEED to take our planet back!

My third *'gift'*.... or *'curse'*.... depending on your point of view, is that **I'm a *Lover*.** I

Planet of the Sheep

love people. All of you. So intensely that I suffer when you suffer. I have been *'blessed'* with extremely high empathic abilities. So much so that I've actually become a self-imposed recluse in order to escape the inundating inflow of emotion. There's a lot of suffering going on right now. I'm feeling it. My recent research has indicated that a huge percentage, a majority of society, is living in fear or pain or some combination of the two. The fear and pain are contagious. To an empathic person, it's like the suspense accompanying a never-ending horror movie nightmare where you desperately want to wake up and can't. Reverse insomnia!

For years, I've been working on techniques to manage my *'ability'* and recently have stumbled upon the tools that not only allow me to re-emerge, but that allow us all to overcome the pain and fear so we can effectively address and eliminate the present and escalating tyranny that threatens our health, happiness, and ultimately, survival.

After all, the bad guys only care about themselves, their *'gang'*, and their reign. They're the *'wolves'*! They have their own

Planet of the Sheep

vision for the future. Their agenda spells: *"get all you can, while you can"*. By selfishly consuming and accumulating, they're generating a carbon footprint the size of Antarctica.

What about the rest of us? The other 6.99 billion..? Scootch over and make some room!

Have I mentioned that we NEED to take our planet back..? Have I mentioned that we can and we will!?

Planet of the Sheep

"As in George Orwell's "Animal Farm": The mission statement has been ever so gradually tweaked over the years that we didn't even notice the 'pigs' moving into the 'big white house'..."

Chapter 2:

The State of the Union

(a little bit about us)

I don't need to belabor all the minute details of the *"problem"*. In fact, volumes have been written on the subject. I went to our local used book store and found the most overwhelming political science section. I couldn't even read all the titles let alone make so much as a dent in reading the books themselves. What I did learn from perusing this collection as well as the new book stores, the library, the internet, and countless interviews and conversations, overheard as well as engaged, was that the problem is huge, complex, totally identified, and very much *un-untangleable* (spell checkers beware).

The problem has been thoroughly identified. The *'seeds'* of revolution have already been planted. The world climate has watered and fertilized those seeds, and the little *'sprouts'* are beginning to show.

You hear it everywhere you go, from

Planet of the Sheep

the highly educated political analyst to the ignorant armchair politicians absorbing media rhetoric as if it were gospel. The people *(sheep)* are seeing through the hypnosis. Through the *'wool'.* So, what IS this *"problem"* I'm talking about?

The *'bad guys' (I'm not being gender specific, they include men and women)*, which I'll now refer to as the *'wolves'* are getting sloppy and tipping their hand. Getting greedy. Getting careless. Getting fat, useless and out of control. Soon we will have no money left, no soldiers *(children)* left, no reputation worth salvaging left. Our tyrannical *(yes let's drop the gloves)* government is being used to lull us into slavery. All along the way the original *"Constitution"* and *"Bill of Rights"* have been *'adjusted'.* As in George Orwell's *"Animal Farm":* The mission statement has been ever so gradually tweaked over the years that we didn't even notice the *'pigs'* moving into the *'big white house'...*

Maybe the biggest *'adjustment' (crime)* was the **enactment of income tax**. It started back in *1913* when *'they'* realized *'they'* couldn't pay their way anymore. It

Planet of the Sheep

started out small and apparently reasonable but, like a *'snowball'*, it's now crushing the life out of us.

To get right to the point, the governments, American AND Global, have outgrown their usefulness. They have grown bloated, self-serving and self-sustaining yet produce almost nothing constructive. They only oppress, control, spend and hoard.

Politicians and corporate leaders live lives of leisure on exorbitant ***six and even seven figure salaries*** while producing literally nothing tangible or constructive. The rest of us work ourselves to death in service and support of them for pitiful wages that won't even begin to meet our basic needs.

This imbalance is not only affecting individuals, entire cities and even states are going bankrupt. Is anyone else alarmed that California, reportedly the seventh wealthiest *'country'* in the world has allowed its coffers to run dry..?

The *'wolves'* spend trillions on wars that can't and won't be won, **EVER**. They blatantly throw away our resources while we hypnotically deny that we are in trouble or

Planet of the Sheep

controlled.

The real scary part is that IF the government continues on its present course of unrestrained growth and grows larger than the general populace, we run the very real risk of having this *'slave'* society become a reality. My biggest concern is that we may have already passed that **'point of no return'**.

All of this reminds me of an old *"Star Trek"* plot. One society enslaving another and over generations both forgetting that it was ever anything other than a symbiosis. Basically a mass hypnosis... like what we have now. Call it *'brainwashing'*. I call it **"slavery"**. Let that one roll around in your mind for a bit. Then let it into your heart. Do you know this to be true?

This is a good spot to include a segment from the *'War Made Easy'* film that amused AND alarmed me. A perfect example of the 'doubletalk dialogue' that 'DC' delivers:

Donald Rumsfeld: "There are known knowns. There are things we know we know. We also know there are known unknowns. That is to say, we know there are some things we do not know. But there are also unknown unknowns, the ones we don't know we don't know..."

These clowns are getting rich and powerful thinking this... 'stuff' up...!

Speaking of D.C... How many times have we been WARNED, by *experts,* about heavy concentration of power and wealth..? Washington DC is a 'powder-keg' sitting on a match.   It's an insatiable monster... a gigantic 'wolf cave'. I'm actually surprised it hasn't already consumed itself from within. It survives... and thrives... because WE let it! We *'feed'* it.   DC will be our undoing left unrestrained. Guaranteed.

Planet of the Sheep

"Does a butterfly flapping its wings in Washington cause a tornado in Toledo..?"

-Confucius *(on a slow day)*

Chapter 3:

Critical mass

(a trip to the crystal ball)

"The end is near!" We've heard it for years... decades... centuries for that matter. We read it in the *"Bible"* and we see it on the back of the *"Eat at Joe's"* placard out on the sidewalk. But it doesn't end. We wait. We prepare. We surrender. We live. We love. We die. But the world keeps turning. Well, my friends, the *'end'* isn't near, it's here. It's a process, not an event. We are currently living/experiencing the fall of civilization. It's incremental. A slow disintegration.

And it's **not happening *'naturally'*.** It's being strategically and carefully planned and implemented. The *'wolves'* have a suicide pact. Whether conscious or unconscious, they have pooled their resources to get what they can, while they can. They know that their time is limited. The clock is ticking. The planet is exhausting. The people *(sheeple)* are coming out of their *'trance'*. The *'wolves'* know this and don't want it. **We're their *'free lunch'*.** Why would they willingly give that up? They won't. They're addicted. Addicted to getting something for nothing.   Addicted to power and control. Addicted to violence, war, and oppression. Like a drug, they need it. They think they need it to survive. **They've even *'brainwashed'* themselves! How ironic.**

It's spinning out of control.   We're reaching a form of critical mass.   Call it *'reverse critical mass'.* **Our society is *'bottoming'* out.**

At this point, allow me to describe the *'funnel effect'*.   Life is about choices. Usually there are a lot of them. We pick and choose and sometimes they're good choices and sometimes not. There are too many. It's hard to pick. Over time, the choices narrow down and after enough time goes by they boil down to two.   At that point, we choose between them. The hitch is…. there's actually always a third choice which is NOT to choose at all. Regardless of which of the three are picked, the funnel phenomenon happens. We pop through the narrow opening which, like an hourglass, is only capable of letting one *'choice'* through at a time. Once on the *'other side',* lo and behold, we have a whole new

Planet of the Sheep

plethora of choices. And the process begins again. Over and over. But each evolution of the process is guided by the choice that was made at the funnel aperture. It's kind of like the science fiction concept of parallel universes and timelines that we're all familiar with. I won't elaborate, but it becomes very clear that every choice we make in life has the potential of a runaway snowball. A *'butterfly effect'.* The question still remains unanswered: Does a butterfly flapping its wings in Washington cause a tornado in Toledo..? More on the *'funnel'* later.

So, what's with this reverse critical mass business? Simple, our global society is using everything up. In our fear of loss, we've been programmed *(I wonder by whom...)* to get what we can, while we can, however we can. Sound familiar. It's a recurring theme so get used to it.

The biggie is the economy. **We're in a recession/depression/over-inflation...** whatever you want to call it... that's making The Great Depression of *1929* look like a picnic. Is that scary? I don't have any money, assets, or investments, and I'm even scared. Those that do *'have'* are scared to

Planet of the Sheep

death. In some cases, literally. From the escalating cost of fuel to the mortgage crisis, from the broken stock market with no substance to support it to the government *'printing press'...* self-explanatory. We're in serious trouble. And no one is providing any hope or solution. It's become a *free-for-all...* more like a *free-for-some...*

Next point: we're always in a war that has no end in sight and it's bleeding us dry. Now, I'm viewing this from an American (an embarrassed and ashamed American) point of view, but with the influence the U.S has *'imposed'* on the world, we have to look at the big picture. **The global picture.** From now on!

The United States of America.... self-appointed *'World Cop'* is *'out of order'*. And needs to be put out of the *police* business.

Don't get me wrong, I'm not a traitor or unpatriotic. I'm a world patriot. A *human* race patriot. No country, culture or organization has the right to impose its policies and beliefs on others. Yet this imposition is the unwritten mission statement of the U.S. government. It's wrong and it's going to stop! Does everyone realize that **the U.S. military currently *'occupies'* about 135 countries!** Those are staffed bases in almost every country in the world... Why..? This *'butting in where we don't belong'* behavior along with our *'superiority complex'* is the second biggest reason for war... profit and greed being the frontrunner. And all fueled by fear. ...Plus we're ignoring and neglecting our own problems right here at home! The money and resources go out there, even to our *'enemies'*, while our own citizens go broke, homeless and starve...

Government leaders worldwide are in fear of losing their positions. Their free ride. Their *'cash cow'.* American leaders aren't the only guilty parties here. All of the governments on earth are perpetuating this *'competition'.* And all under the guise of protecting their people. Are YOU feeling safe and protected..?

Face it people, we're being converted into slaves. Reduced to *'lambs'* bred for slaughter and consumption. We're basically a commodity... but, luckily, a necessary one to the *'wolves' (this being our temporary saving grace).* Not a pretty picture at all. Let's

Planet of the Sheep

stand up together and take our lives back! We can if we lose our fear and rebel.

I could go on talking about scary stuff indefinitely, but I promised I wouldn't so allow me wrap this up with just two more important points.

First, a thought provoking viewpoint on our supposedly severely broken educational system. How did it get broken? Is it broken..? Or has it been converted into a *'brainwashing'* (brain*dulling*) factory? They call them *"public schools"*. Truth be told, they're actually government schools. It's no wonder they're failing. It's planned. They're **'dumbing down' our kids** so they won't figure out the situation. After all, they are the next generation of slaves. The writing is on the wall... for those who can still read...

The second point has to do with our *yummy* fluoridated water. It has come out in my research that fluoride is only good for teeth in children ten years old and younger. It does nothing for older teeth. So why is it in our city water supplies countrywide? Could it be because fluoride is the main ingredient (94%) in Prozac..?! This drug is not only

Planet of the Sheep

used to treat depression, it renders the user docile... it kind of suppresses the rebel in you. I, personally, don't drink the stuff... **The 'wolves' are incrementally and methodically 'brainwashing' AND drugging us into submission. Dumbing us down mentally AND physically**! Let THAT 'soak' in for a minute...

Back to this issue of critical mass. It's rapidly coming to a head. Our fragile infrastructure, our shaky economy, our peace of mind *(or lacking thereof)* is leading to social breakdown and outright chaos. *Where is Maxwell Smart when we need him..?*

The U.S. seems to always be on the brink of, yet another, exorbitantly expensive, useless and even comical presidential election. Another no win scenario. Another futile four to eight years of lies, deception, greed and impotency. And if someone outside the *'wolf pack'* is elected, God help them. The bad guys just won't tolerate it... just like back in *1963* with JFK, the last honest U.S. President. Look at history... this shouldn't be too tough, we keep repeating it. But that's for another chapter.

Planet of the Sheep

Another mixed blessing in the critical mass equation is technology. It's great and it's not. On the positive side, it makes our world very comfortable and efficient. Communication and computing are screaming forward. Transportation is becoming state of the art. And the *'toys'...* THAT list is endless.

But the negatives are huge too. The war machine, which is sucking up most of the money *(not creating it as we're led to believe)*, has technology that is virtually unbelievable... and soon to be obsolete *(as soon as we 'outlaw' war)...* AND that money, like all those lives, civilian and military, is gone. Irretrievable.

The entertainment industry is gradually phasing out actors and replacing them with that phenomenal CGI *(computer generated imagery)* that we're all becoming addicted to. Have you tried to view an old movie lately? Kind of requires a little patience, doesn't it?

And then there's you kids and young people. I know you love your games and phones and laptops but did you know there is a plethora of studies out there currently classifying you as the ***dumbest***

generation?! *(see further research)* I'll leave you to read that book on your own... **if** you can still read. Are you offended? I would be too. Don't like that label? Only YOU can change it. And I'd seriously consider doing just that... before you can't... I, personally, am alarmed and disappointed because I was looking forward to YOU becoming my future leaders instead of those old farts that are dumbing you down so you can clean their toilets and flip their burgers.

I could go on and on forever on the subject of high tech but I think I've made my point. I like it too but it also alarms me. So I'll get back on topic...

The *'window'* is rapidly approaching if not already here. A *"funnel"*. Are you ready to choose to reclaim our world? Or will we surrender it again? This IS a choice to be made. Choose wisely!

The purpose of this plan is to have something viable and feasible in place for when *'we'* finally DO hit bottom. A plan with a purpose to fill the void created by the coming period of confused or perhaps absent leadership if not to replace the present

Planet of the Sheep

regime of corrupt and irresponsible *overlords*. A plan with a new vision of hope for a milked and crushed civilization. A plan that requires everyone's participation. The world is vulnerable. Our society is primed for change as our whole economy *rollercoasters* and flies off the tracks. Frightened? Join the revolution and have not only *'a new hope',* but a solid purpose in life that will contribute to saving your world.

A New Hope. This is not a new concept. There's an old movie about rebellion with that very title... In fact, it's a whole saga that parallels our current society with frightening similarity. And let's all hope AND pray that this mess we're in doesn't spread to the *'stars'* and mess them up too! If it does, the *'wars'* surely WILL never end. ...I hope *George* won't mind the references as I use his material a lot...

One Silicon Valley billionaire is funding a potential project to create floating libertarian *'countries'* in international waters. These 'floatopias' will supposedly be free of all these present terrestrial problems. My take on this idea is this: *"you can run but you can't hide"* and *"who gets to live there and who chooses?"* What's to prevent these human problems from migrating there too? ...They never got solved. No, if this idea actually comes to fruition, a good strategy would be to have all the *Globalist elites* move there to be one big happy family and leave the rest of us on land to sort out their mess and get back to living life. Speaking more pragmatically, shouldn't all that money be spent on the ultimate solution rather than on a temporary crackpot scheme... *a band-aid..?*

Very Important Note:

I've just revealed the **'tip of the iceberg'** *in this chapter. I SO highly recommend that you* **read the book titled "The Trillion Dollar Conspiracy"** *by* Jim Marrs 2010, that I *prescribe it as* **mandatory reading**. *His resources are extensive and he has refined the information into a clear, concise and very readable format. Even if you just* start *reading it, you won't be able to stop. He gives ALL the details. I* guarantee *you will get so* 'worked up' *that you won't be able to resist joining the* 'revolution'!

Remember those *'bad'* Borg villains from *Star Trek* who preached... "resistance is

Planet of the Sheep

futile" *and* "prepare to be assimilated"..? *This couldn't be more true... today... in REAL life!*

Question is: Will you join (or be enslaved by) the endangered evil "Empire", or embrace the strengthening benevolent "Rebellion"...?

PICK UP 'THE TRILLION DOLLAR CONSPIRACY'!!   YOU WON'T BE ABLE TO PUT IT DOWN!!

IF VIDEO IS QUICKER FOR YOU, WATCH 'ENDGAME'...

Consider this your first homework assignment...

Chapter 4:

Birth of a Revolution

(your mission when you accept it)

So! What do we do about it? War suggests that both sides stand an equal chance of winning. This, assuming the *'deck'* isn't *'stacked'*. In a revolution, WE can *'restack'* the *'deck'* too...

We KNOW we need to take back our planet. But how? A whole sector of the population is contributing to the cause already. *"Do your part"*, or *"Be the change you want to see in the world."* Or how 'bout the latest and very controversial **'Occupy Movement'?** Good in concept. Lacking in strength, coverage and immediate productive value.

There are a lot *of 'do-gooders'* in the world... from wealthy philanthropists to the bum on the street recycling our careless discards. It just won't be enough. We need full participation in the saving of our world. Even the *'wolves'* will require rehabilitation and re-assimilation into society.

Planet of the Sheep

The key to the success of this plan is that **no one gets left out or left behind.** Everyone gets to come to the feast. There's enough to go around with plenty left over. The rich can stay *(miserably)* rich. The poor can stay happy AND finally have enough. Confused? Have you talked with any happy, content rich people lately..? Usually the happy ones are the ones that are helping the destitute and underprivileged. Giving *'it'* away so to speak.

With global peace *(due to the absence of government intervention/regulation),* our society will take care of itself. Guaranteed. It's human nature. We don't need a 'babysitter' anymore. We're all *'grown up'.* It's time to retire the *'sitter'.* Agree? This so-called *'retirement'* is not going to be an easy transition... for ANY of us. People naturally resist change. This is why the brainwashing is so effective. We would rather succumb than *'do the work'.* We're afraid to risk our fragile *security (I say that word through squinty eyes)* in favor of taking a chance on human nature. That *'nature'* being one of love, caring and nurturing. It's pretty effective *'brainwashing'* to actually make us believe that slavery is in our best interest or that warmongering is the true root of human nature. It's even working against our basic instincts. The government has mastered this skill. This ability to use fear and misinformation to manipulate us into doing their bidding. We will kill and/or die for our government. And we do this on a regular basis under the delusion of patriotism. This is the business they're in. And war is big business. That's why we've always had it. This is why good presidents have been murdered over it... and will continue to be. This is why **EVERY American President since JFK has outright lied to us.** They're ALL in the war profiteering business.

Coincidentally, or not, I'm currently editing this chapter on 9/11/11, the tenth anniversary of you know what. It is with a very heavy heart and all due respect that I lay this one on you... For those who haven't already figured it out *(and most of you actually have),* the *World Trade Center fiasco (911)* was absolutely an inside job, a controlled demolition. Simply Google *"911 Inside Job"* and be overwhelmingly convinced that the *official* story is a complete *'snowjob'.* The indisputable FACTS are all there. But the frustration is how do you go about

Planet of the Sheep

prosecuting your own government. They're kind of in charge... for now... Our own government demolished those buildings and murdered our loved ones with forethought, intention and malice to manipulate our hearts into supporting a war with no end. A war against an enemy that not only didn't do it, but an enemy that our own 'trusted' leaders created! This is only one example in a whole chain of similar episodes in our violent history. I don't know about you, but I'm extremely disturbed by ALL of this.

No... war and violence are NOT human nature. They are simply a byproduct of greed using fear and hate as the catalyst. Using our hearts to support this cause is the embodiment of evil.

John F Kennedy was the last TRUE antiwar president. A real 'lion'. I guess the rest learned their lesson from HIS fate. They joined the 'wolves'. The 'pack' looks out for their own. I believe the current U.S. President, Barrack Obama, may be a 'lion' but, surrounded by 'wolves', is not able to implement the degree of change promised and required to 'swing the pendulum'.

Planet of the Sheep

Onward to the plan.

So, why aren't all these little changes and contributions adding up and fixing our world? Don't the *do-gooders* out-number the *bad guys?* Aren't there more *'peaceniks'* in the world than *'warmongers'..?* I would LIKE to think so.

Allow me to quote one of my idols and mentors who, I believe, is far ahead of his time and far more enlightened than many give him credit for: ***"Don't underestimate the power of the dark side".*** I know most of you figured that one out. And for those who didn't, ask your kids... you know, those little people who are supposed to *(and deserve to)* inherit a decent, functioning planet. They'll know.

The evil that pervades and operates in our lives is very powerful. One evil deed can wipe out a whole squadron of good deeds. They don't play fair. They don't have rules *(morals).* Once again, refer to that *'galaxy long ago and far away'.* A metaphor, yes. But a good one. If you need a real example, go back to *1939* where one isolated source of pure evil, Adolph Hitler, corrupted and

Planet of the Sheep

hypnotized a whole nation of good, loving people. Either on a whim or planned, matters not, he recruited them to join his cause (Nazism) and, using fear and hate as the catalyst, mobilized these good intentioned, normal folks to rise up and perpetrate one of the most massive, hideous crimes against humanity in world history. One of. This is only one of countless examples but I think the point is clear.

If evil IS in charge AND is more powerful, what chance do we stand? How can we extinguish it? If what we're doing isn't making a dent, what else is there? It's time for another story... another metaphor:

One of my favorite old *John Wayne* movies is titled *"Hellfighters"*. It's about an elite group of oil well fire fighters that go all over the world putting out these enormous, dangerous fires. We still have these fires and these heroes today in real life. Take a look at *Kuwait* in *1992*.

As an aside, as this is a perfect place in this story to give honorable mentions: Don't we currently know and believe that our *(non-corrupted)* fire fighters, police and soldiers are the true heroes in our society today? Look at the *World Trade Center* disaster for that proof, as well as all the *unjustified wars* they've fought and died in for us. Unfortunately, these examples also prove my point about evil still overpowering good.... which gets me back on point...

The oil fires are tricky little devils. They need to be *'blown'* out... similar to blowing out a candle only on a massive scale... with explosives. If everything isn't perfectly timed and executed, the fire will simply re-ignite. If the superheated debris isn't cleared *(during the blaze),* and the explosive charge isn't cooled during insertion into the inferno, the fire won't go out or will go out and then re-ignite. It's ALL about timing and positioning.

Similar to our current situation in the world. We go around snuffing out the little insurrections and dethroning petty tyrants thinking we're making a difference. Electing the most convincing promise makers *(breakers).* All from our hypnotized and drugged mental state with the hope of getting positive results. Recycling little bottles and cans, while the warmongers are nuking our

Planet of the Sheep

neighbors and burning holes in the atmosphere. Our small efforts are with good intentions and they're a good start. But they'll never be enough to reverse the momentum of the destroyers. We need a bigger 'stick'. A better *weapon*. **A weapon of "mass construction".**

Did you get that? A *weapon* that **creates rather than destroys.** If hate is the *weapon* that destroys, can you guess what the *weapon* is that creates, that heals, that provides real security. It's a *'no-brainer'* and I really feel that I'm insulting your intelligence if I say it. So it's your guess. A hint: it's also a four letter word. And too simple to be true. But is.

But, *(and this is the biggest BUT),* it won't work without perfect timing and execution. Otherwise, the fires of hate will re-ignite and we'll be right back where we started. **Living out history... over and over and over and over...... till we run out of it...**

It is a requirement for the fulfillment of this plan, that everyone eventually be *'on board'.* Involved. Willing to risk everything

Planet of the Sheep

for peace and security and a saved world. Even you *warmongers...* I suspect and sincerely hope that you're reading this too... After all, what good is a burned up *dirt clod* of a planet full of *rebellious slaves* to you..? You NEED to be *(and will be),* convinced that it is in your best interest to convert to peace. That you can still *'have'* without *'taking'.* And, in the process, you'll learn that *"Having is not as good a thing as wanting. This is not logical, but often true".* Did I just quote another genius..? As long as I'm on a roll, how bout this old favorite: *"The needs of the many, outweigh the needs of the few... or the one."* and I'll add my own ending: *"...or the wants of ANY".*

So there you have it. A simple solution to a very complex problem. Simple in concept, but complicated in execution. I guess I'll have to write some more. I love this planet AND all of its inhabitants. **We need to save this world, for everyone's sake!** WE. ALL of us.

Food for thought for you *'wolves'*: *"ALL"* includes YOU! Yes, you're wanted and needed. And loved. Without us *'lions'* and *'sheep'*, you would only have each other.

Planet of the Sheep

And, whether you believe it or not, you need us too. A planet full of *'wolves'* would be boring at best and a terrible nightmare at worst! *'We'* enhance *'YOUR'* world... and you KNOW it!

This brings to mind the television reality show *"Survivor"* where contestants ally with one another to eliminate the others. In the end, and quite logically, these alliances collapse as they turn on one another in the final scramble for the coveted title of *"Sole Survivor"*... a prestigious but lonely pedestal. **A lot of money but no friends seems like a losing proposition to me...**

A *'lone wolf'* or a planet full of happy, friendly *'party animals'*... You don't even need a brain to know this choice is a *'no brainer'!!* Come on 'wolves', get a clue... ***Join the party, you're invited.***

Chapter 5:

A Call to Action

(execution without death)

How? What are the *weapons* we'll use? What are the actual steps we'll take to neutralize these *'bad guys'*? How will we reverse the *'brainwash'*? Attain *sobriety*? How will we convert the greedy *warmongers?* This *"weapon of mass construction" (WMC)*, where do we get it, how do we learn about it and how to use it? I'm glad you asked. Are you ready for a little adventure outside of the *'nine dots'*? Buckle up.

Unconventional. This will be the theme of this chapter. Many of you will recognize these concepts. Most of you will be uncomfortable with them. This is OK. I'm here to introduce you. To give you a comfort level. To convince you that this is the only way we're going to get our society back on its feet.

To begin: ***There will be NO violence.*** First and foremost. **Absolutely none.** We'll call it *"Passive Non-Compliance".* This is

Planet of the Sheep

about a PEACEFUL rebellion... we already KNOW *(from* thousands *of years of experience)* that violent ones NEVER work. **A revolution without bloodshed and casualties.** Something similar was attempted back in the '60's and '70's but failed due to lack of proper *'weaponry'* namely hindsight and knowledge. All that drug use and abuse probably didn't help either... The *'rebels'* had the *'love'*, they just didn't have the numbers, the organization and the *'critical mass window'*. Remember, timing and execution are everything. There was passion and vision, but this wasn't enough to overcome the *'big wheel'*. The revolution fizzled and the wheel rolled on.... right over us.... *squish!!*

What's different now? We have the numbers, we have the *'tools'*, we have the knowledge and experience, and most important, we're reaching a point where most, if not all, hope has been exhausted. This *lack of hope* is what I keep referring to as the *'window'*. It's also very important to point out that, as in the *"funnel"* illustration, there's only going to be one choice to be made in this *'window'*. One shot at freedom. If we don't act in this imminent *'window'* of opportunity, we will be condemned to yet another reign of oppression and tyranny that we simply won't survive. All indicators point to **this being the LAST window**. Our last chance.

I think many are beginning to *'get this'* already. The current *'Occupy'* movement, which is highly reminiscent of the *'sit ins'* of the *70's,* is rapidly becoming stronger and very much reflects the attitudes and desires of our hurting and awakening *(as it has been so aptly labeled)* "99%". There is already controversy over this movement, however, and care must be taken not to let it take on enough negative press to get it *'squashed'*. Also, it's a great start but won't be nearly enough to achieve our ultimate goal of global revolution and takeover. Still, I like the sound of ***"Global Occupation". "GO" for short***. This is absolutely going in the right *(as in correct)* direction. We're just going to take it to the highest level... To make it the ***"100% Solution"*!**

Another question popped into my mind that you may be thinking: Isn't it dangerous or even foolhardy, to reveal our plan to the *'enemy'*? The answer to that is an adamant

Planet of the Sheep

NO! Remember, we're operating *'outside of the box'*. Secrecy has been used before and failed. Besides, there IS no real *human* enemy.

Now this part is the most important part of the plan. Get this if nothing else! The enemy here is fear. I'll repeat: **FEAR IS THE ENEMY**. Get that straight and we're on the road to success. To true freedom.

With this in mind, it's time for another lesson. This might turn into a *'long and winding road'* so, again, fasten your seat belts. I'm going to belabor this definition of the *'enemy'*. Fear. We all have it... on some level. It's a *human* thing, and there's been no getting around it... until now.

The whole foundation of the philosophy of the *"Course in Miracles"* boils down to one basic concept. So very simple. ***Fear vs. love.*** They are polar opposites. They cannot co-exist in the same moment. They both live inside us, but we can't embrace them simultaneously. Some people get real close, but no one achieves this. It's like oil and water. They simply don't mix. Experiment with this if you choose, argue with it if you must. But when you finish, you may just reach the conclusion that the confusion it produces borders on insanity. This is precisely why our society is more and more rapidly going insane. The **humans are confused.** They are constantly attempting to manage and balance this confusion without truly understanding its core nature. The simplicity of the solution is magnificent and beautiful. Elegant. And totally freeing.

But before you learn where the fear comes from, see where it leads. The most important factor in warfare is to **understand the enemy**. Without this understanding, the battles and ultimately the war are lost before they even begin.

Are you still with me..? How 'bout a story? I just love that shrimpy 800 year old 'goblin'. He said that *"fear leads to anger, anger leads to hate, hate leads to suffering, and suffering leads to the dark side"*. Well, there's something that he left out till Episode 3, the last Star Wars film, that is the *'crux of the biscuit'*, the *root* of the problem. That being, **where does the fear come from?**

The answer to that question was what

Planet of the Sheep

brought the solution to my attention in a magnificent epiphany I had during my research. Fueled by an extremely enlightened church leader from a poor African country who came to my town in the U.S. to speak to us about peace, I was completely *'bowled over'* and the entire solution *'clicked'* at that moment. You see, we *NEED* to understand where the *fear* is coming from! Back up the train. Address the cause. No more *'bandaids'*. No more placebos. Focus on the cure... on a total healing.

Here it comes... **"LOSS leads to fear".**

Since we were little children, we have experienced loss. Then fear was *'born'*. The example the lovable African used was this: *"When your young child came up to you wearing your grown-up clothes, what was your response? You, most likely, exclaimed: "Oh, you beautiful child, how wonderful you look wearing daddy's shoes!""* (chuckling and most heads nodding in the audience). *"You just ruined your child".* (the chuckling stops, the heads stop nodding, the jaws drop to the laps). *"You see, your child just 'lost' his identity. Now he believes he isn't beautiful*

Planet of the Sheep

unless he's in someone else's shoes. His own shoes are inadequate. He proceeds to carry this belief through his childhood and on into adulthood. It infects other aspects of his life. He compensates in many varying ways but ultimately doesn't recover because he's lost his identity and doesn't even realize it let alone have the skill set to reclaim it. He becomes dysfunctional in an unlimited variety of ways. And to think how simple it would have been to just tell the small child: "NO, don't wear daddy's shoes, you're absolutely beautiful in your own"".

But, as parents, we didn't know this. Nor did our parents. And theirs. It's commonly referred to as *"the sins of the fathers".* Bad teaching passed down through the generations. No one at fault, it just is what it is. But it doesn't have to be anymore. Ah, the power of knowledge...

Loss comes in many forms. Loss of people, loved ones and love; loss of money, possessions and security; loss of mental ability, loss of youth, loss of life. Loss of identity and self esteem, as mentioned in the 'story'.

Planet of the Sheep

Those are some of the *'biggies'*. Some of the more subtle ones may include anything from losing a great parking space to something as ridiculous as losing a car length on the highway! I KNOW you all experience that one... I see it EVERY day and have seen it escalate to extremely violent cases of *'road rage'*. All that danger and stress in the interest of shaving a couple of seconds off your travel time... which you end up giving back a hundredfold at the very next red traffic light anyway..! So we actually fear losing the limited commodity of **time.** I, personally, haven't mastered this yet. It takes effort and patience. MY biggest fear is losing my *'sheep'...*

Loss comes in many forms, but it **always leads to fear.** Now, are your getting intimately acquainted with the *enemy?* We're *'afraid'* of what we'll *'lose' (or not have),* so we grab up everything we can.

Well, with everyone *'grabbing',* we get *angry.* It's a frustrating competition thing... maybe natural, maybe learned. Doesn't matter, it simply is.

When we realize that our *anger* doesn't

accomplish anything productive, we slip into *hatred*. We *hate* the futile competition as well as the relentless competitors. But *hate* is an emotion. It only affects *(injures)* the person generating it. Frustration ensues as results are not achieved. The festering *hate* needs to escape. Soon, it manifests itself through behavior. Either *aggression* or *suffering.*

Now, I've never known *hate* to generate good behavior. It's simply not logical. The *hate* always leads to bad, misguided, criminal, violent, immoral, etc. action or, simply to *pain*. To the *'dark side'* so to speak. *The end of the chain. The end of peace, love, and harmony.*

So, how do we *'nip this in the bud'*? How do we repair the damaged *'roots'*? Again, SIMPLE: **Eliminate the sense of loss.** Restore people's identities... and stop destroying them to begin with. This goes for their CULTURES TOO! Educate people about death and dying and relationships. Provide lasting security through natural *human* communion as opposed to artificial government oppression *(babysitting)*. Nurture and heal the sick and feeble instead of abandoning them. Practice better time management so the roadways can be an efficient and pleasant experience as opposed to a *'demolition derby'!*

My favorites: **Get everyone involved.** Get them on 'purpose', on a mission of service. Get them passionate about making a difference! The list goes on and I'll let you think up your own. I think the concept is clear.

The bottom line is that ***"there's enough to go around... with too much left over".*** There is absolutely no excuse for and no place for a *'have/have not'* class system. We take *everyone* to the top. We eliminate the *'lost'* concept altogether. Everyone gets *'found'.* Everyone *'has'.* And greed will be extinguished. Why bother, there's already too much surplus. Everyone will be rich. Financially, emotionally, spiritually and socially. **Problem solved.**

Back to the subject of the big business of war. The weaponry we now possess and have so expensively paid for, can destroy the planet 100 times over, this we know. Do we realize that the same money *(trillions to date)* can, or could have, **healed the world... 100**

times over? The cost of the present war alone could have eliminated all world hunger, educated everyone, provided free health care for life for everyone and, most important, reduced the price of gasoline to five cents a gallon... OK, that last one was a *little bit* exaggerated...

Truth is, if we *'fire'* most of the government and their corrupt corporate *(war industry)* *'tagalongs'* and *boycott the petroleum industry,* we could begin to embrace all of the sabotaged, repressed and misrepresented alternate fuel sources and eliminate the reliance on stealing from our neighbors... **the very roots of war.** Also, we would *stop 'bleeding'* the resources of our fragile planet... **the roots of extinction.** Coming full circle yet..? Need more convincing? Maybe later.

For now, **back to the solution.** Loving, sharing and serving. **Sharing.** I used to tell my materialistic little toddler: If you share, you get twice as much stuff, not half as much AND, as a bonus, someone to play with too. I don't think she got it but that's a different story...

Planet of the Sheep

As for the big picture, hopefully it won't be as challenging to convince whole countries of this concept. Think about it, the U.S. has too much food and not enough oil. The Middle East has too much oil and not enough food. Am I the only one that sees through the fog here..? Is it so simple that we can't accept it? Now, I get to ask a question: Why do *humans* always have to make *'rocket science'* out of everything? Why does it have to be complex in order to be important or have impact? The theory of *'Occam's Razor' (Law of Economy)* is about simplification. That whatever the *simplest* solution is probably IS the correct and most efficient one. More on sharing in Chapter 7 and 8.

Now it's time to go metaphysical on you. Quantum physical. The new science. *'Woo woo'* stuff. Time to teach you the most powerful WMC in our arsenal. **Energy.** And NOT the kind you get in an energy bar or drink. Not the kind that runs your toaster or blows up a whole city. This is the type that can be tapped into and manipulated with thought and intention. We don't realize how close *Obi Wan* was when he taught *Luke* about it. In fact, if you choose to call it the *'Force'*, you wouldn't be too far off.

Planet of the Sheep

According to the proven theories of quantum physics, all matter in the universe consists of miniature energy packets. Nothing is solid, not even rocks or people. Even thought is energy. As a result of this simple concept, energy can have an effect on energy. Guided energy can influence other energy. If you follow this through to its conclusion, thought can manipulate matter. Mind over matter..? We used to call that science fiction. I'm happy to say: *"The times they are a changin'"*.

Energy healing has been around for a long time. In more recent years, it has found its way into western culture. About ten years ago, I discovered its miraculous abilities. It led to the saving of my best friend's life. A little over ten years ago, I read the supposed work of fiction, the *"Celestine Prophesy"* by *James Redfield 1993* and followed up with its sequels. It was interesting but was before my exposure to *'the real thing'*. This last year, I've reread the *'Insights'* of the prophesy and I have to say, they have a whole new *flavor (impact)*. Earlier, I mentioned finding the tools to help me re-assimilate into society. To assist me with my *'feeling too much'* problem. The *'insights'* were my answer.

Planet of the Sheep

The mixed blessing is that everyone has the ability to manipulate energy. Most just aren't aware of it. The result is that there is a constant *(unconscious)* battle for it. A giving and taking that happens subconsciously. This is the biggest cause of strife in human relationships. And most of us don't realize it's happening. It simply happens, and then we wonder why we *'feel'* good or bad. We're all inadvertently affecting each other. An example of when it's good is when you walk into a room or party or event populated by happy people, you get uplifted. You match the *'energy'* in the place. An example of when it is bad is when you're in a hurry on a crowded road with a group of similar *'stressed out'* people. The result can be anywhere from more stress to aggression and rage. Sometimes (more and more often these days) the *'road rage'* actually leads to physical violence. This escalation, this *'downlift'* is caused by mishandled energy, or what we'll call *'bad energy'*.

For a GREAT, super-simplified explanation of quantum physics and the whole energy phenomena, check out the video: *"What the Bleep Do We Know!?, Down the Rabbit Hole" 2004.* The graphics are a kick too. It's very entertaining and educational.

Here's the concept that really *'got'* me. Energy can also be projected. Across space AND time... at least across time into the future. This is the foundation for the entire *'secret'* of manifesting (see the book and video, *"The Secret"*).

Again, good or bad energy can be projected. And projecting can also be done consciously OR unconsciously. Most of it is being done beneath the level of consciousness. This is why we have war, violence, hate and on and on. It's also the reason we don't even realize why we're doing the *'bad deeds'*. We just do them and then **rationalize or excuse but never truly understand.**

We also subconsciously *'cause'* good things to happen. These we *'write off'* to luck. Are you getting all this? Are you *epiphanating* yet..? Are you ready to do some thought experimentation and discover your true power?

This energy projection, used positively, is the *'weapon'* we're going to use to fix our world. I'm depending on ALL OF YOU to use your new found powers responsibly and beneficially. Remember the spider who learned that with **great power comes great responsibility...**

And for those who choose to use your new skills for evil, understand this: this is one arena where good and evil ARE balanced. You WILL be outnumbered and you'll be wasting your time and your energy. You WILL be overpowered and rendered impotent. So don't even bother... as I'm sure the *troublemakers* will eventually discover.

I continue to address *'the troublemakers'* because there will be a period of adjustment *(while the 'brainwashing' wears off)* where the *'wolves'* will resist peace. Remember, *warmongering* is an addiction.

Also, as a side note, know that addiction is a result of making a *choice,* NOT a *disease.* I know that I'm going against modern day addiction theory, but that's my own *'out of the nine dots'* opinion and experience.

Now for something else *'outside of the box'* for you to ponder: Have you ever heard

Planet of the Sheep

of *"consensus reality"?* This is one of the foundational theories behind quantum physics. It also ties into energy projection. You see, we all decide, as a group, what our reality will be and it miraculously comes true. It manifests. Examples: We've always been in a state of constant war. Most of us believe this is just the *'natural way of man',* and so that's what we get. Similarly, we decide we want more and better technology. Lo and behold, it *'shows up'!* We believe there's a plague, we get one... a big one. We believe the sky is blue and the grass is green. We believe *(or are led to believe)* that only fossil fuel can run an engine. The list is endless.

Now that we understand this powerful concept, let's start believing, as a group, in only positive things. No wars, no disease, no hate... But here's a hint, drop the *"no's"* and reframe our phrasing to only positive beliefs. **Peace, health, love...** It is a proven psychological fact that thinking no war is still thinking about war... and so forth. This re-phrasing is crucial. Don't miss this concept. Let's all think into existence a beautiful, fully functional planet and society. A *utopian civilization (See chapter 9. Also see my Asimov reference).*

Planet of the Sheep

There are three terms in the field of energy science that are utilized that are actually very similar. They are **"intention"**, **"expectation", and "assumption".** We must always *'frame'* our thoughts in these contexts. We must constantly monitor our thoughts because *(as previously explained)* our thoughts have power and impact. All of them. We have to **send out** thoughts *(energy)* with intention. Positive intention. We must **receive** energy with a positive expectation. **Expect only good.**

And finally there's assumption. This one has most often been held in a negative light. You know the ditty: *"assume makes an ass out of you and me".* Well, once again, be a turnaround specialist. Make it positive. I see assumption as being very similar to intending and expecting but it takes them to another level. It combines them. This is the future predicting and changing phase of **energy projecting.** The real power. You assume that your goal is already realized... in advance. **The ultimate ability to manifest.** This is how praying works also. Backing up your energy projection with love and prayer *'supercharges'* it!

Planet of the Sheep

This is all covered, quite eloquently, in *Redfield's "The Secret of Shambala, the Search for the Eleventh Insight" 1999.* **Also required reading for *'lions'*!**

There's a famous classic painting titled ***"The Return From Wars: Mars (war) Disarmed by Venus (love)".*** The artist got it right... a long time ago!

Now you are intimately aware of the inner workings of the *peaceful weapon.* The *weapon of mass construction.* Go out and practice. Get good at it. No one is without this ability. Everyone that has a working brain and heart can learn this. Can master this. We need to be *'armed'* for our first, last and only battle. We get one shot. When we hit *critical mass,* we need to strike. We need to *'back-brainwash'* the *bad guys.* I just made that up but it's not too far from the mark.

I remember when I was a kid, a ridiculous idea went around that was something like: if everyone sneezed or yelled or jumped up and down at exactly the same time, the world would shake or something. I don't remember it *exactly* but some of you may. This, of course was meaningless, probably never happened, and would have accomplished nothing. But it illustrates my point. If we all have a *'cue'* to simultaneously project our powerful energy and prayer into society and the planet, like with the oil fires, we will extinguish this whole **'fear polarization'** *loop.* We will tip the balance and *'break the big wheel'.* We WILL take over and reclaim our planet. Save our civilization. Reverse the fall.

How will we recognize the crisis point of the *'window'?* I believe it will be obvious. It may have even been predicted already by those clever **Mayans** a long time ago. As mentioned earlier, a time is coming when all hope will be lost. When the *'you know what will hit the fan'* and chaos is the order of the day. When violent rebellion ensues and the walls of *'authority'* come tumbling down. A cue for everyone to give all your focus right at one specific moment. Like with the oil fire, we want to put this thing out in one blow. **One huge burst of positive, constructive energy that will overwhelm and extinguish the fear once and for all.**

As I fretted over how and when to set

this crucial timing, the solution was delivered right to me. It was when this **2012 Mayan calendar** business came to the forefront. Since *'something'* is supposed to happen at the *Winter Solstace 2012,* why shouldn't it be **our revolution..?** What better time to implement our *'social evolution'?* Rather than have that date pass without so much as a whimper, as did the Y2K (year two thousand) computer breakdown prediction, we can create our own cause and effect. Unless an asteroid kills us all, which would render all of *human* history moot anyway, **why not take control of our destiny?!**

So here it is: At **11:11 AM (UTC/GMT) on December 21, 2012,** everyone send your most powerful blast of energy into the world. With **positive intention, expectation and assumption coupled with intense love and, most important, prayer,** let us extinguish once and for all the flames of fear. Reverse the *'spiral' (see Appendix "B").*

In the meantime, as mentioned earlier,

practice your energy management and master it. Also practice the **'Action Steps'** outlined in *Appendix "A"*. They include more immediate, concrete steps we all can take today **to 'undermine' and 'overthrow' the present tyrannical regime.** If our **'Love Bomb'** fails, which is highly unlikely, our only back up plan is to do this the *'old-fashioned'* way... with *'blood, sweat and tears'...* and failure. Repeating history... again...

I just love the term "NO BRAINER"!

"Go directly to jail, do not pass go, do not collect $200.00!"

-Monopoly

Chapter 6:

Out with the Old

(no encore, please)

Time for a history lesson. My all time favorite *"Bible"* verse is *"Proverbs 26:11".* You'll love this. ***"As a dog returns to its vomit, so a fool repeats his folly."*** What this means in essence is that *'they who do not learn from history are condemned to repeat it'.* This is what's happening with our current political administration as well as the last fifty years or more of it. Seeing the pattern?

Well, I have a theory: If we do only what hasn't been done before, we're on the right track**. This plan is outside of the 'box'. Outside of the 'nine dots'. Unconventional.** Never been tried or done before. To quote the little green philosopher, ***"do or do not, there is no try."*** We're going to *'do'* this, my friends. There will be no *'try'.* Are you game? Anything and everything that has been tried before and has failed, has no place in this plan. This is a plan for success. Not an ongoing encore performance in failure. We're seeing too much failure in the performance of the world's governments and leaders, and we're sick and tired of it. **It's time to run the 'show' ourselves** and run it right! And we can. And we will. *"So it has been written, so it shall be done."*

The first and foremost action required to reel in the government is to stop supporting it. Financially and philosophically. This is going to sound scary and dangerous but believe it, if everyone stopped voting, stopped sending their children to government *(public)* schools, and stopped paying taxes, the *'big wheel'* would come to a grinding halt. Almost instantaneously. **Out of the tyranny business.** Permanently! Nobody would *go to jail.* There aren't enough police or jails to arrest all of us and besides, they would be keeping their hard earned money in their pockets too. **The IRS would be defunct.** The corrupt politicians and *globalists* would be learning some new skills... some productive skills.

We would finally be on our own to grow and flourish. To **recapture our intelligence, our bank accounts, and our**

passion for life. To leave the *'enslavement'* and thrive. And the ONLY thing we would *lose* would be our fear.

Cycle broken, problem solved.

Planet of the Sheep

"...A great set of rules were provided by God".

Chapter 7:

Transitioning

(growing pains)

Rules, rules, rules. What are we going to have for rules? How will we keep order? What about crime? What about the deviants and *bad guys* who don't want go with the program? What about the newly unemployed millions *(hopefully not billions)* of government employees? Everyone from selfish politicians to our brave protective heroes, soldiering in the field? Administrative clerks to judges behind the bench? There will also be the huge matter of *entitlements...* That's the non-producing overhead of pensions, retirements, social security, disability and other awards... *deserved or not...* What about our pretty much destroyed economy? **Good questions.** And worthy of good answers. You shall have them. No mystery to this plan.

Without government it may seem that crime would run amok and justice would be fleeting. Complete lawlessness. Well, isn't it that way now? I won't dwell too much on the broken legal system. That problem has been obvious for all too long. With **hundreds of thousands of laws** in place and more adding to that number every day, a confusion has been provided that *'blurs'* all the lines and creates more opportunity, not less, for criminal behavior. Could this be due to the fact that criminals are the ones making and manipulating the laws..? What a *'racket'* for *'job security'...* And yet one more reference to the *'animal farm' parallel...*

Also, I refuse to spend your precious time on the huge failure of the correctional (prison) system. Again, we need to get out of the short term fix mentality. These problems will automatically sort themselves out once the people are back in charge. As soon as everyone *'has'*, no one will need to *'take'* anymore. Nip it in the bud, folks. Keep it simple. Let's save *'brain surgery'* for brains, not social science... Let's use *'rocket science'* for space exploration, not war machines... Are you getting the theme here?

I mentioned the hopelessly broken economy. I'm not an economist but even I know that this situation is beyond repair. The 'math' is too simple. Sorry. The only solution

Planet of the Sheep

I can come up with is to start over. From *'scratch'...* and whatever that entails. If you have a better one, let us all hear it. But none of that *'same ol'* drivel that we're sick of. Make it new and innovative. It's GOTTA be *'out of the box'.* It HAS to be feasible and do-able. Duhhh!!

Even in the ***'brave new world'*** that we're envisioning, a society of peaceful anarchy *(don't be intimidated by this word),* there will need to be some rules to live by. I can think of a few: How 'bout *"live and let live",* or *"thrive and let thrive".* Then there's the classic *"Golden Rule"...* you know it... *"Do unto others as you would have them do unto you".* That one might get a little *'slippery'* considering people's varying preferences in what they would like to have *'done'* to themselves...

A great set of rules were provided by God. And they're very simple. If we adopted the Ten Commandments, we'd be done. They pretty much cover all the 'bases'. I will take a moment to list them for your edification. I'm not pushing religion. I, personally, think these are very simple, clear and logical:

ONE

Love your creator...

(whichever YOU choose)

...and love each other

(all the humans)

TWO

Don't let materialism replace #1

(see above)

THREE

Don't use foul language, especially aimed at #1

FOUR

Take a day off each week to rest

(best prevention/cure for illness and insanity)

FIVE

Honor your parents

(best way to STOP the 'sins of the fathers' syndrome)

SIX

Don't murder

(do you REALLY need this one explained!)

SEVEN

Don't commit adultery

(it CAN lead to #6, see above)

EIGHT

Don't steal

(won't need to, you'll already 'have' everything)

NINE

Don't lie

(honesty IS the best policy! Why settle for second best..?)

TEN

Don't covet

(again, won't need to. Your neighbor will share it anyway)

Did you enjoy that? I had fun spicing them up a little, but the concepts are clear... and pure. I will never, ever push religion on anyone. I don't evangelize and won't. Everyone is free to believe however they wish. I DO know that studies show that **99% of society believe in God** in some form. This is good. This should be our ONLY form of accountability! Society *(our new 'gang')* will *police* the remaining 1%. And I don't mean through lynching and abandonment. We will rehabilitate the few remaining *'troublemakers'* with *love* and a sense of belonging. We will help them to **lose their sense of loss.** How's that for a *paradoxical conundrum?* Sorry, I've always wanted to say that in public.

Planet of the Sheep

Another potential set of rules could be the *"Bill of Rights"* and the *"Constitution of The United States"*. This is considerably less appropriate because they were designed and implemented long ago to keep government governed. **Basically to put a governor on the government.** Whew! Another mouthful. And more government than I can stomach in one paragraph! With the disbanding of the *'wolf pack'*, the *"Constitution"* becomes irrelevant, obsolete. So I'll leave that one in the *'recycle bin'*.

I know! Let's talk about the ***"Declaration of Independence"!*** This we CAN use. But let's draw up a new modern one, to fit our plan for freedom. We'll keep it simple... our new *'mantra'* if you haven't caught on yet... Here's a **sample** of how our new declaration should read:

"We the People of the planet Earth do hereby declare our total and complete freedom from the tyranny, oppression and control provided and imposed by the governments and elites of the world. We, as a group, fully take on the responsibility as loving, caring, social beings to govern ourselves and to care

for and nurture those who can't or won't. We vow to share all that we have and produce and to serve others whenever possible or feasible. We declare love as our global belief system. Our only political policy is peaceful anarchy with leadership provided by all. Our new single political affiliation shall be named the Co-Manifest Party. Our mission statement, platform, is to manifest peace, love and harmony. We hereby declare that we, as a global community of unique and independent nations, will continually excel in the maintenance and enjoyment of the Utopia that we have created. Sign below."

Hmmm, I haven't quite figured out how to get 6-7 billion signatures in one place... This will just have to be a good starting point for practicing the *'honor system'...* our new philosophy. So, that was our model mission statement. Did I overlook anything?

OK. As promised earlier I'll answer some more questions. I'm really going to *'try'* and be nice here... did I say try..? A major

Planet of the Sheep

challenge will be what will the millions of unemployed government workers and leaders do now..? Got any hobbies? Surely you *'wolves'* must have some skills that don't involve administrating a *'slave planet'.* Our new society is going to have millions of new jobs. We still need to design, build and repair roads, buildings, power sources, hospitals, entertainment facilities, cultural landmarks, etc. The list is endless. There's still going to be research, science, technology, travel, healing, and shuffleboard. We're not going back to the woods... most of us. Back to the dark ages. We still get to keep all the good stuff we have. We're just getting rid of the bad stuff. And the *bad guys.*

The marketplace *(economy)* will be based on **Laissez Faire (free market) Capitalism** where transactions will come back to the level of the individual and away from the convoluted, corporate controlled sector. Trust me on this! We WANT this!!

I'm sure our whole monetary system will have to, somehow, be reinvented from the ground up. ...We've destroyed it that completely! I wouldn't be surprised if we actually go back to a barter system. But who

118

Planet of the Sheep

knows? I don't. What I DO know, and trust, is that *'necessity is the mother of invention'*. Another classic is *'nature abhors a vacuum'*. With all of our unified *'good intentions'*, positive solutions will be uncovered for all of these difficulties and challenges. The TRUE *human* way!

With the elimination of fear and oppression, we will finally be able to thoroughly enjoy the *'fruits'* of our labor. I don't know about you, but **I've been waiting far too long for this.** Unemployment will be obsolete. There will be enough for everyone... especially enough things to do.

For more ideas and elaboration, check out another genius far ahead of his time, Isaac Asimov. His book *'Robot Visions'* is a brilliant collection of short stories and essays. Two essays stood out that address this subject FAR more eloquently than I ever could. They are "Whatever You Wish" 1977 and "Future Fantastic" 1989. **Required reading for *'lions'*.**

Planet of the Sheep

Warning: if you are currently employed by, sponsored by, contracting with, or literally running a government somewhere in the world, start thinking about and planning what you want to do next. The *'free ride'* is over. We're not going to *'feed'* you anymore. Start dreaming. Embrace the *'vision'*. The sky's the limit. And, start now. Time is preciously limited.

We want you to join our gang.

Chapter 8:

Paradigm Shift

(keeping the peace)

How will we keep our hard earned, long awaited peace from *de-volving* back into the state of chaos it was? What kind of maintenance will be required for a peaceful, non-warring planet? Sound like a *'no-brainer'*? It actually is! There's and old acronym, perhaps the oldest, *K.I.S.S., "Keep It Simple, Stupid".* I personally don't like that one. Especially seeing that with the abolition of government schools *(and government period)*, we won't have stupid people anymore. I've revamped it to say **"Keep It Simple, Share."**

What a perfect segue for another story: *"What I did last summer."* I went to Panama and visited two peaceful tribes of Indians. One lived in *'apparent'* poverty on a series of hundreds of tiny islands. The other lived deep in the jungle and had a simple existence... wait a minute... they weren't existing, they were living. Simply. What the two tribes have in common is that they have

Planet of the Sheep

no government *(to speak of),* and they share. They're happy and content.   Basically crime free. Fulfilled. **They have mastered peace.** I felt guilty that we were coming into their world *(as tourists)* and exposing them to *"the evils of capitalism."* Showing them evidence of the big world *'out there'* and corrupting their core culture.   Also, I felt torn because I have *'things'* that they don't.   Things.   Wait just a darn minute, they were happier and more content than I've ever been in my whole materialistic life.   What an epiphany!   After mopping away my tears, I declared "I'm staying here!"   Then, I thought about it and came to the realization that I could never move there.   I'm addicted to my stuff.   I needed to go home and be unhappily surrounded by my junk.   I revised my statement to say: "I wish I was born here" so I could experience that peace too. Since time travel hasn't been invented, I surrendered to the fact that there would have to be another way to find *their* peace in *my* world.

Here's the clincher: **peace is contagious!** I came home and couldn't rest. Couldn't stuff the *'cat back into the bag'*. I'd been *'infected'*. The goal of this little story *(huge, actually)* and of this plan, is to infect

Planet of the Sheep

YOU! To **infect the world.** With an infection that will kill the 'cancer' that's killing us all. Maybe 'antidote' is a better use of language, but you get the point.

Think about it a minute. For the first time in history, the world is at peace. Totally without war. Everyone has their 'dream come true'. Sharing is the order of the day. No one is bored or without purpose. We're all contributing and benefiting from our God given talents and enjoying those of others. **A global healing.**

And think of the diversity. Once we quit trying to conform the planet to one political philosophy, or religion, or culture, or currency, or language, or lifestyle, or whatever (did I really just say WHUT EVRRRRRR?), think how fun and interesting it will be.

Tourism will be at an all time high and terrorism non-existent. Terrorists want to have love and families and fun and safety too. And can. Of course, you're going to have to choose new occupations too... peaceful ones.

And we can choose to relocate

Planet of the Sheep

anywhere we desire. If you don't like where you live, move. If you're jealous of what America *'has'*, move there! Don't *'blow it up'*! If you DON'T like living in America, leave. It will all sort itself out as you go where your HEART leads you... **not** your fear. Without immigration laws and political borders, we can unabashedly explore and experience our wonderful world and society. We can travel and settle where we wish. And adapt to whichever culture we choose to inhabit.

All the varying cultures of the world will remain healthy and intact. Ah variety... Truly the **'spice of life'.** As opposed to greed, fear, hate and war, the *'poison of life'* and bane of our existence. Does this sound appealing..? Now THAT was a ridiculous question.

Hopefully, soon, I can go hang out with my *'friends'* in that Panamanian jungle tribe after all! I've already packed my toothbrush, Visine, and loincloth...

Chapter 9:

A New Eden

(life in the garden)

What can be said that hasn't already? We're now spiritually and socially evolved. We have our dreams, our happiness, our peace, our security, and all those new friends. What a party! **We survived and conquered the Mayan prediction!**

But we're a *'restless animal'*. We are always on the move. Always growing, learning, inventing, exploring... And mostly, loving. What WILL the next frontier be? You choose. Lie around in a hammock in the woods, or command a starship where no one has gone before. Anything and everything is possible.

Just do the *"Quantum Thingy"*.

Planet of the Sheep

"...*the* 'military industrial complex', *if left unrestrained, would run amok and consume us...*"

-Eisenhower's farewell address

"We didn't listen and consequently didn't '*fare*' very '*well*'..."

-A Rebellious Lion

Epilogue

Utopia def. U•TO•PI•A (Yoo•**Toh`**•Pee•*uh*) n.
1. Any visionary system of political and/or social perfection, 2. An ideal place or state, real or imaginary

Since the beginning of *'civilization' (I use that term lightly),* battle and war have been the prequel AND the sequel to battle and war. War has always been (completely unsuccessfully) used as a mechanism for finding/creating peace. What a gargantuan irony. Worse still, a belabored exercise in absolute futility. It has NOT worked... EVER! Do you think maybe it will in the future..? I'm not holding my breath on that one. Be it in literature or reality, we have always had war. We've never experienced a lasting period of peace. To quote a thought provoking line from the excellent film, *"War Made Easy, How Presidents and Pundits Keep Spinning us to Death",* "War becomes perpetual when it's used as a rationale for peace".

War will never go away unless a completely unconventional, untried approach is incorporated.

Planet of the Sheep

It has been postulated that we actually NEED war. Some arguments in favor of war are that it boosts the economy or that it is a form of population control. Some just say that it's basic *human* nature. What a *'snow job'* to beat all. An enormous *'money pit'.* And senseless waste of human potential. What a waste of human spirit as well as precious life. But most important. war and violence are the polar opposites of peace, love and harmony.

'They' say ***"War is big business".*** There's NO question regarding that! Do you ever ponder if peace can be big business too..? There's no doubt we're deeply entrenched in the *'wrong program'.* And if *'business'* is SO good, why is the global economy crippled? Could it be that those war profits are being pocketed somewhere..? No *"could be"* about it! You do the *'math'...*

In President Eisenhower's farewell address *(very well presented in the award winning film, "Why We Fight" by Eugene Jarecki)*, he adamantly warned us that the *'military industrial complex'*, if left unrestrained, would run amok and consume us. We didn't listen and consequently didn't

Planet of the Sheep

'*fare*' very '*well*'... Now war profiteering is the '*order of the day*'. A great fiction example of this would be Tony Stark in the sci-fi story, "*Iron Man*" but for a very real example, look to the Halliburton scandals and their ties to the U.S. Presidency.

In the corporate sector, what better examples than the Enron fiasco or the whole petroleum industry monopoly..? Are you familiar with the film about the true story of "*Who Killed the Electric Car?*" It doesn't take an '*Einstein*' to figure THAT one out!

It is going to require a gigantic commitment and effort to break free of this *(multi)* millennia old situation. The concept of "*utopia*" is fleeting and far-fetched at best. Unless, as a species, we don't unanimously embrace and work towards creating it, it will elude us and we will forever be condemned to repeating some very old and very ugly history. History that I, personally, am disgusted, embarrassed and fed up with.

Come on humans, we're smarter than this!

Planet of the Sheep

"Just DO It"

-Nike

Afterword

(back to the parable)

So! Where did you end up? *'Lion'* or *'sheep'*? Both are good choices. Based on the psychology of *"A"* type and *"B"* type personalities, there are always going to be *'leader'* types and *'follower'* types. Aggressive and passive personalities. Active *'lions'* and lazy *'sheep'*. Neither are better or worse. They just are. There will be no judgment. No crying *"not fair"*. Remember, it's all about choices. Everyone gets to choose, and everyone will be accepted. Nobody wins until everybody wins. If you resent the *"B's"*, then become one. Likewise with the *"A's"*. This is too simple and logical to be argued. Just *'be'* what you want to be. Zero competition... except in sports and games... the only place where it belongs.

I'm a *'lion'*. Often I get overwhelmed by our predicament and want to become a *'sheep'* and just graze. But I can't unlearn what I've learned. I can't forget. Therefore, I'm committed to my *'lionhood'*... my *'pride'*... and our mission to dethrone and rehabilitate the *'wolves'*.

Planet of the Sheep

"For every action, there is an equal and opposite reaction..."

-Sir Isaac Newton

Appendix A

Action Steps

Take your children home out of the government *(public)* school system.

(Re)educate yourself and your kids. Knowledge and truth are power.

Plant a *'victory garden'* and lessen your dependence on the marketplace.

Spread the message of the revolution to everyone.   We NEED everyone.

Break the 'news habit' the corporate media is owned and *'shaped'* by the *'bad guys'...* the *warmongers.* It does NOT reflect reality... just agendas.   The news is also known to be a huge source of depression and basically *'fuels' 'crisis mode'!*

Stop paying taxes that *'fuel'* the broken system and keep the *'wolves'* fat and powerful. Pay only for what you believe is needed to further positive and PRODUCTIVE results. This will invariably end up in the private sector... which, ideally, will end up being the only sector... *COOL!* Paying for *'butter'* rather than *'bullets'*... *Sign me up!!*

Stop voting and supporting criminals and their greedy, extremely expensive, self-serving issues and agendas.

Arm yourself! That means own firearms AND plenty of ammunition and know how to use them. You won't ever shoot anyone but you'll need them just the same. THIS ONE IS IMPORTANT!!

Practice wielding your energy as you're going to be using it... a **LOT.** THIS ONE IS VERY IMPORTANT!!

Change your mindset and make the conscious decision to love and not focus on loss. Reverse the *'spiral'*.

Embrace Laissez Faire (Free Market) Capitalism and boycott

corporate monopolies and government sponsored... anything. Become a *'flea-rat'...* Flea *(and farmers)* markets and Swap Meets are where it's at! Try it!! Buy AND sell... reduce your 'stuff level'... see Appendix "F", *the Earth is Full.*

Be aware and beware that there

actually IS a very powerful group of individuals that have a long-running master plan to subjugate us. Expose them and we disarm them as their biggest weapon is secrecy.

Be ready to embrace a big, positive

change. It's been emptily promised to us for decades. Now we're going to manifest it ourselves. Still, it won't be easy.

Know that you're not alone

in your fear and dissatisfaction. There are millions of us already working towards the illusive *'utopia'.*

Avoid violence at all costs. It hasn't, doesn't and won't work. Non-violent non-compliance is our strategy. Love and energy are our weapons.

Embrace and convert the warmongers and money grubbers. They are disillusioned and worthy of forgiveness and assimilation into our new joyful world. We're all messed up human beings on some level. Our mission is to get EVERYONE un-messed up.

TAKE ACTION don't sit back and wait for the world to change. You won't like what you get. BE the change you want to see in the world. It's ALL about manifesting!

Actively manifest peace, love and harmony.

Appendix B

The Love/Fear Spiral

The 'Light' comes from *peace and joy.*

Peace and Joy come from *harmony.*

Harmony comes from *service.*

Service comes from *sacrifice.*

Sacrifice comes from *love.*

Love comes from a *decision, a choice.*

Loss leads to *fear.*

Fear leads to *anger.*

Anger leads to *hate.*

Hate leads to *suffering.*

Suffering leads to evil and violence,

...The 'Dark Side'...

Planet of the Sheep

"So It Has Been Written, So It Shall Be Done"

-Charlton Heston

Appendix C

The Ten Laws *(Commandments)*

ONE

Love your creator...

(whichever YOU choose)

...and love each other

(all the humans)

TWO

Don't let materialism replace #1

(see above)

THREE

Don't use foul language, especially aimed at #1

FOUR

Take a day off each week to rest

(best prevention/cure for illness and insanity)

FIVE

Honor your parents

(best way to STOP the 'sins of the fathers' syndrome)

SIX

Don't murder

(do you REALLY need this one explained!?)

SEVEN

Don't commit adultery

(it CAN lead to #6, see above)

EIGHT

Don't steal

(won't need to, you'll already 'have' everything)

NINE

Don't lie

(honesty IS the best policy! Why settle for second best..?)

TEN

Don't covet

(again, won't need to. Your neighbor will share it anyway)

Appendix D

The New Declaration of Independence

We the People of the planet Earth do hereby declare our total and complete freedom from the tyranny, oppression and control provided and imposed by the governments and elites of the world. We, as a group, fully take on the responsibility as loving, caring, social beings to govern ourselves and to care for and nurture those who can't or won't. We vow to share all that we have and produce and to serve others whenever possible or feasible. We declare love as our global belief system. Our only political policy is peaceful anarchy with leadership provided by all. Our new single political affiliation shall be named the Co-Manifest Party. Our mission statement (platform), is to manifest peace, love and harmony. We hereby declare that we, as a global community of unique and independent nations, will continually excel in the maintenance and enjoyment of the Utopia that we have created. Sign below.

Appendix E

The "E" Listers

24 Attributes evident in every 'Lion'

Ecstatic	Enlightened
Educated	Enraptured
Effectual	Enterprising
Elastic	Entrepreneurial
Eloquent	Essential
Emissary	Ethical
Empathic	Excellent
Empowered	Exemplary
Enduring	Expansive
Energetic	Extraordinary
Engaged	Exuberant
Enhanced	Evolved

Appendix F

I feel compelled to include this very appropriate and alarming *New York Times* article from 2010 by Thomas Friedman:

The Earth is Full

You really do have to wonder whether a few years from now we'll look back at the first decade of the 21st century –when food prices spiked, energy prices soared, world population surged, tornados plowed through cities, floods and droughts set records, populations were displaced and governments were threatened by the confluence of it all – and ask ourselves: What were we thinking? How did we not panic when the evidence was so obvious that we'd crossed some growth/climate/natural resource/population redlines all at once?

"The only answer can be denial," argues Paul Gilding, the veteran Australian environmentalist-entrepreneur, who described this moment in a new book called "The Great Disruption: Why the Climate Crisis Will Bring on the End of Shopping and the Birth of a

Planet of the Sheep

New World." "When you are surrounded by something so big that it requires you to change everything about the way you think and see the world, then denial is the natural response. But the longer we wait, the bigger the response required."

Gilding cites the work of the Global Footprint Network, an alliance of scientists, which calculates how many "planet Earths" we need to sustain our current growth rates. GFN measures how much land and water area we need to produce the resources we consume and absorb our waste, using prevailing technology. On the whole, says GFN, we are currently growing at a rate that is using up the Earth's resources far faster than they can be sustainably replenished, so we are eating into the future. Right now, global growth is using about 1.5 Earths. "Having only one planet makes this a rather significant problem," says Gilding.

This is not science fiction. This is what happens when our system of growth and the system of nature hit the wall at once. While in Yemen last year, I saw a tanker truck delivering water in the capital, Sanaa. Why? Because Sanaa could be the first big city in the world to run out of water within a decade. That is what happens when one generation in one country lives at 150 percent of sustainable capacity.

"If you cut down more trees than you grow, you run out of trees," writes Gilding. "If you put additional nitrogen into a water system, you change the type and quantity of life that the water can support. If you thicken the Earth's CO_2 blanket, the Earth gets warmer. If you do all these and many more things at once, you change the way the whole system of planet Earth behaves, with social, economic, and life support impacts. This is not speculation; this is high school science."

It is also current affairs. "In China's thousands of years of civilization, the conflict between humankind and nature has never been so serious as it is today," China's environment minister, Zhou Shengxian, said recently. "The depletion, deterioration and exhaustion of resources and the worsening ecological environment have become bottlenecks and grave impediments to the nation's economic and social development." What China's minister is telling us, says Gilding, is that "the Earth is full. We are now using so many resources and putting out so much waste into the Earth that we have reached some kind of limit, given current technologies. The economy is going to have to get smaller in terms of physical impact."

We will not change systems, though, without a crisis. But don't worry, we're getting there.

We're currently caught in two loops: One is that more population growth and more global warming together are pushing up food prices; rising food prices cause political instability in the Middle East, which leads to higher oil prices, which leads to higher food prices, which leads to more instability. At the same time, improved productivity means fewer people are needed in every factory to produce more stuff. So if we want to have more jobs, we need more factories. More factories making more stuff make more global warming, and that is where the two loops meet.

But Gilding is actually an eco-optimist. As the impact of the imminent Great Disruption hits us, he says, "our response will be proportionally dramatic, mobilizing as we do in war. We will change at a scale and speed we can barely imagine today, completely transforming our economy, including our energy and transport industries, in just a few short decades."

We will realize, he predicts, that the consumer-driven growth model is broken and we have to move to a more happiness-driven growth model, based on people working less and owning less. "How many people," Gilding asks, "lie on their death bed and say, 'I wish I had worked harder or built more shareholder value,' and how many say, 'I wish I had gone to more ballgames, read more books to my kids, taken more walks?' To do that, you need a growth model based on giving people more time to enjoy life, but with less stuff."

Sounds utopian? Gilding insists he is a realist.

"We are heading for a crisis-driven choice," he says, "We either allow collapse to overtake us or develop a new sustainable economic model. We will choose the latter. We may be slow, but we're not stupid."

...More 'food for thought'...

Appendix G

The Lord's Prayer is all about manifesting:

*It's about ACTION **not** ASKING. Notice that intention, expectation and assumption are all emphasized...*

Dear Father in Heaven, hallowed is your name.

(this covers at least 3 love commandments...)

Your Kingdom come, your will be done,

(expectation of utopia via the Creator's perfect master plan)

on Earth as it is in Heaven.

(our present mess will be repaired and we will live in joy)

Give us this day our daily bread,

(our needs and wants will be met)

Planet of the Sheep

And forgive us our sins as we forgive those that sin against us.

*(we get to **have** 'do (it right) overs', we get to **give** 'do (it right) overs')*

Lead us not into temptation and deliver us from the evil one.

(guide us into good choices and protect us against bad ones)

For yours is the Kingdom, the Power and the Glory, ...and the Grace,

(we don't have to be in charge of the tough stuff, it's handled...)

Forever.

(long term fix, no 'band-aids')

Amen

(it is so...)

Appendix H

'Heal the World' Michael Jackson

little girl talking:
(I think about the generations
and they say they want to make it
a better place for our children and our children's
children
so that they know it's a better world for them
and I think they can make it a better place)

There's A Place In Your Heart
And I Know That It Is Love
And This Place Could Be Much
Brighter Than Tomorrow
And If You Really Try
You'll Find There's No Need To Cry
In This Place You'll Feel
There's No Hurt Or Sorrow

There Are Ways To Get There
If You Care Enough For The Living
Make A Little Space, Make A Better Place

Heal The World
Make It A Better Place For You And For Me
And The Entire Human Race
There Are People Dying
If You Care Enough For The Living
Make A Better Place For You And For Me

If You Want To Know Why
There's A Love That Cannot Lie

Planet of the Sheep

Love Is Strong It Only Cares For Joyful Giving
If We Try We Shall See
In This Bliss We Cannot Feel Fear Or Dread
We Stop Existing And Start Living

Then It Feels That Always Love's Enough For
Us Growing So Make A Better World
Make A Better World...

Heal The World...

And The Dream We Were Conceived In
Will Reveal A Joyful Face
And The World We Once Believed In
Will Shine Again In Grace
Then Why Do We Keep Strangling Life
Wound This Earth Crucify Its Soul
Though It's Plain To See
This World Is Heavenly
Be God's Glow

We Could Fly So High Let Our Spirits Never Die
In My Heart I Feel You Are All My Brothers
Create A World With No Fear
Together We'll Cry Happy Tears
See The Nations Turn Their Swords Into Plowshares

We Could Really Get There If You Cared Enough
For The Living
Make A Little Space To Make A Better Place...

Heal The World...
...Make A Better Place
For You And For Me

Appendix I

'Imagine' John Lennon

Imagine there's no heaven
It's easy if you try
No hell below us
above us only sky
Imagine all the people
Living for today

Imagine there's no countries
It isn't hard to do
Nothing to kill or die for
And no religion too
Imagine all the people
Living life in peace

You may say I'm a dreamer
But I'm not the only one
I hope someday you'll join us
And the world will be as one

Imagine no possession
I wonder if you can
No need for greed or hunger
A brotherhood of man
Imagine all the people
Sharing all the world

You may say I'm a dreamer
But I'm not the only one
I hope someday you'll join us
And the world will live as one

Further Research and Viewing

*Priorty   **Read First

Good Stuff Section:

*Imagine *(song)* John Lennon

*Heal The World *(song)* Michael Jackson

*What The Bleep Do We Know!? *Down the Rabbit Hole (film) 2004 (great Quantum Physics for the layman! MUST VIEW)*

*The Holy Bible *(books, films, audio)* ...at least *start* reading it... start with the Gospels. It IS the true 'manual for life'... believe or not... *(required)*

*Quantum Touch, *The Power to Heal* (book & videos) Richard Gordon 2002 *(energy basics)*

The Secret, *Everything is Possible, Nothing is Impossible* (book & **video) Rhonda Byrne 2006 (great manifesting concepts!) *(required)*

*The Celestine Prophesy *(book 1993 & **video 2005**)* James Redfield (learn energy theory and management)

The 10th Insight *(book)* James Redfield 1997

Planet of the Sheep

**The Secret of Shambala, The Search for the 11th Insight *(book)* James Redfield 1999 (advanced energy management, social evolution)

*The 12th Insight *(book)* James Redfield 2011 (bringing it home... up to now)

*Declaration of Independence 1776 *(required)*

*U.S. Constitution 1787 *(required) (kinda dry)*

*U.S. Bill of Rights 1789 *(required) (dryer still)*

*Robot Visions *(book)* Isaac Asimov *(short stories & essays) I recommend these two essays:* **Whatever You Wish** *1977; and* **Future Fantastic** *1989 (absolutely visionary!)*

*The Aquarians, *An Ancient Mayan Prophesy – A Modern Phenomenon 12/21 11:11 2012 (book)* Eric Rankin 2008 *(a nice novel... do dolphins play a bigger role than we know..?)*

A Course in Miracles *(book & program)* Helen Schucman & William Thetman (& Jesus) 1976 *(great study of fear, love and forgiveness)*

*A Shepherd Looks at Psalm 23 *(book)* w. Phillip Keller 1988 *(great study in sheep psychology) (required reading for lions)*

The Dancing Wu Li Masters *(book & audio) Gary Zukav 1979 (quantum physics, heavy science*

Planet of the Sheep

stuff... not for the 'light' reader)

*Divine Intuition *(book)* Lynn A. Robinson M.ED. 2001 (this is a beautiful book!)

*Hope For The Flowers *(book)* Trina Paulus 1972 (about conformity and transformation, absolutely whimsical and delightful)

*Follow Your Heart, *Finding Purpose in Your Life and Work (book)* Andrew Matthews 1999 (great book about figuring out what you want to do...)

*Star Wars Saga *(books & videos)* George Lucas & Lucasfilm 1975 to present; *various quotes from Yoda. (many parallels to our own civilization)*

Star Trek *(books & videos)* Gene Roddenberry 1966 quotes from *"Amok Time"* & *"The Wrath of Khan"*

Lord of the Rings *(books 1955 & films 2001)* JRR Tolkien (there is also a good National Geographic special comparing the novel to our present day world)

Planet of the Sheep

Bad Stuff Section:

**The Trillion Dollar Conspiracy, *How the New World Order, Man-made Diseases, and Zombie Banks Are Destroying America (book)* Jim Marrs 2010 *(required)*

*Animal Farm *(book & films) George Orwell* 1945

*Cheque Mate, *The Game of Princes, The New World Order: Dark Conspiracy or Benevolent Master Plan How it Affects You and the Sovereignty of America (book)* Jeffrey A. Baker 1993 *(reads like yesterdays news...) (required)*

*Chaos Point, *The World at the Crossroads (book)* Ervin Laslo 2006 *(7 Years to Avoid Global Collapse and Promote Worldwide Renewal)*

*The Truth, *What You Must Know Before 12/21/12 (book)* Steven Hawley Martin 2008 *(required) (could be in the 'good stuff' section...)*

*Taking America Back, *A Radical Plan to Revive Freedom, Morality & Justice (book)* Joseph Farah 2003 2005 *(required) (a valid Christian viewpoint)*

*Google: *'911 Inside Job' for you-tube videos*

**Endgame, *Blueprint for Global Enslavement (film)* Alex Jones 2007 *(required) (compelling evidence of the 'genocide plan'...alarming!)*

Planet of the Sheep

*War Made Easy, *How Presidents & Pudits Keep spinning us to death (book & film)* Norman Soloman 2006 *(required viewing) (very revealing government 'brainwashing' strategies)*

*The True Story of The Bilderberg Group *(book)* Daniel Estulin 2009 (wanna know names? This book will give the elitist who's who lists)

*911 Inside Job, *Unmasking the 911 Conspiracies* *(book)* Jim Marrs 2004 *(required) (the truth is way more believable than the official cover (up) story!)*

The New World Order *(book)* Pat Robertson 1991

Why We Fight *(film)* Eugene Jarecki *2006 (includes Eisenhower's farewell address footage)*

The Coming Anarchy *(book)* Robert Kaplan 2000

Global Capitalism *(book)* Will Hutton and Anthony Giddens 2000 (articles & opinions)

*The Dumbest Generation, *How the Digital Age Stupifies Young Americans and Jeopardizes Our Future (book)* Mark Bauerlein 2008 2009

1984 (book & films) George Orwell 1949

Brave New World *(book) Alduous Huxley* 1931

Planet of the Sheep

*Who Killed the Electric Car? *(film)* Chris Paine 2006 (the 'petro' monopoly gaveth/taketh away!!)

The Fog of War *(film) Errol Morris* 2003 *(Best Documentary)*

The Secret KGB JFK Assassination Files *(film) Hosted by* Roger Moore 2000

*The Great Un-gun Debate, *Live from London (film)* 2004 *(in the Library of King's Collage)*

The Bible Code III, *Saving the World (books)* Michael Drosnin 2010

*The Day after Roswell *(book)* Philip Corso 1998 *(the truth is 'out there')*

Why Do People Hate America? (book) Ziauddin Sardar, Merryl Wyn Davies 2002

101 People Who Are Really Screwing America *(book)* Jack Huberman 2006 (basher book)

101 Ways America is Screwing Up the World *(book)* John Tirman 2006 (basher book)

Steeling the Mind of America *(book) (transcripts from the conference)* 2005

Steeling the Mind of America Vol. II *(book)* 2006

One Crazy Bibliography!

Contact information and book orders:

www.lions-unite.org

Clover Publishing

THIS BOOK WILL SAVE YOUR LIFE!

It's about reclaiming our increasingly deteriorating civilization through non-violent rebellion and revolution.

We're in trouble! You KNOW this, I don't need to sell it. Are you unemployed? Losing your house? Unable to gas your car? Are you hungry? Is watching the news getting you down? Is it getting you nowhere? Or... do you just have a **bad feeling** about your world but don't quite know why?... which is where I started. You could be in a position where you have your needs and wants met but are witnessing the implosion of the lives of those you know and love or even strangers. Wondering if and when it will affect you too... Then there's the unenviable position of being one of the *bad guys' but* feeling guilty. Worst case... are you a *bad guy* AND simply don't care?

Chances are you are in the list above in some variation or combination. We all are. And take notice that NONE of the above are desirable positions. This is simply because a *broken world* is **no fun** for anyone!

This book is about rebirth, second chances, getting a 'do over'! It's about *'frolicking in the garden'* as opposed to *'crawling in the desert'*. It's about:

Learning, living and loving!

Contact information and book orders:

www.lions-unite.org

Clover Publishing

Made in the USA
Charleston, SC
17 February 2012